HERO² SQUARED

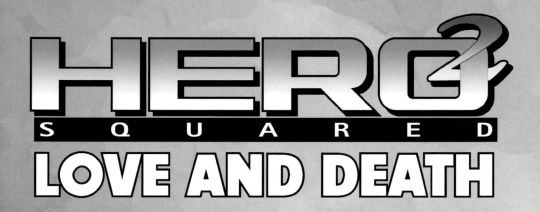

LOVE AND DEATH

ANDREW COSBY
ROSS RICHIE
founders

MARK WAID
editor-in-chief

ADAM FORTIER
vice president,
new business

CHIP MOSHER
marketing &
sales director

MATT GAGNON
managing editor

ED DUKESHIRE
designer

Hero Squared: Love and Death — published by Boom! Studios. Hero Squared and all Hero Squared content is copyright © Keith Giffen and J.M. DeMatteis. Boom! Studios™ and the Boom! logo are trademarks of Boom Entertainment, Inc., registered in various countries and categories. All rights reserved. The characters and events depicted herein are fictional. Any similarity to actual persons, demons, anti-Christs, aliens, vampires, face-suckers or political figures, whether living, dead or undead, or to any actual or supernatural events is coincidental and unintentional. So don't come whining to us.

Office of publication: 6310 San Vicente Blvd, Ste 404, Los Angeles, CA 90048-5457.

First Edition: June 2009

10 9 8 7 6 5 4 3 2 1
PRINTED IN KOREA

CHAPTER 1

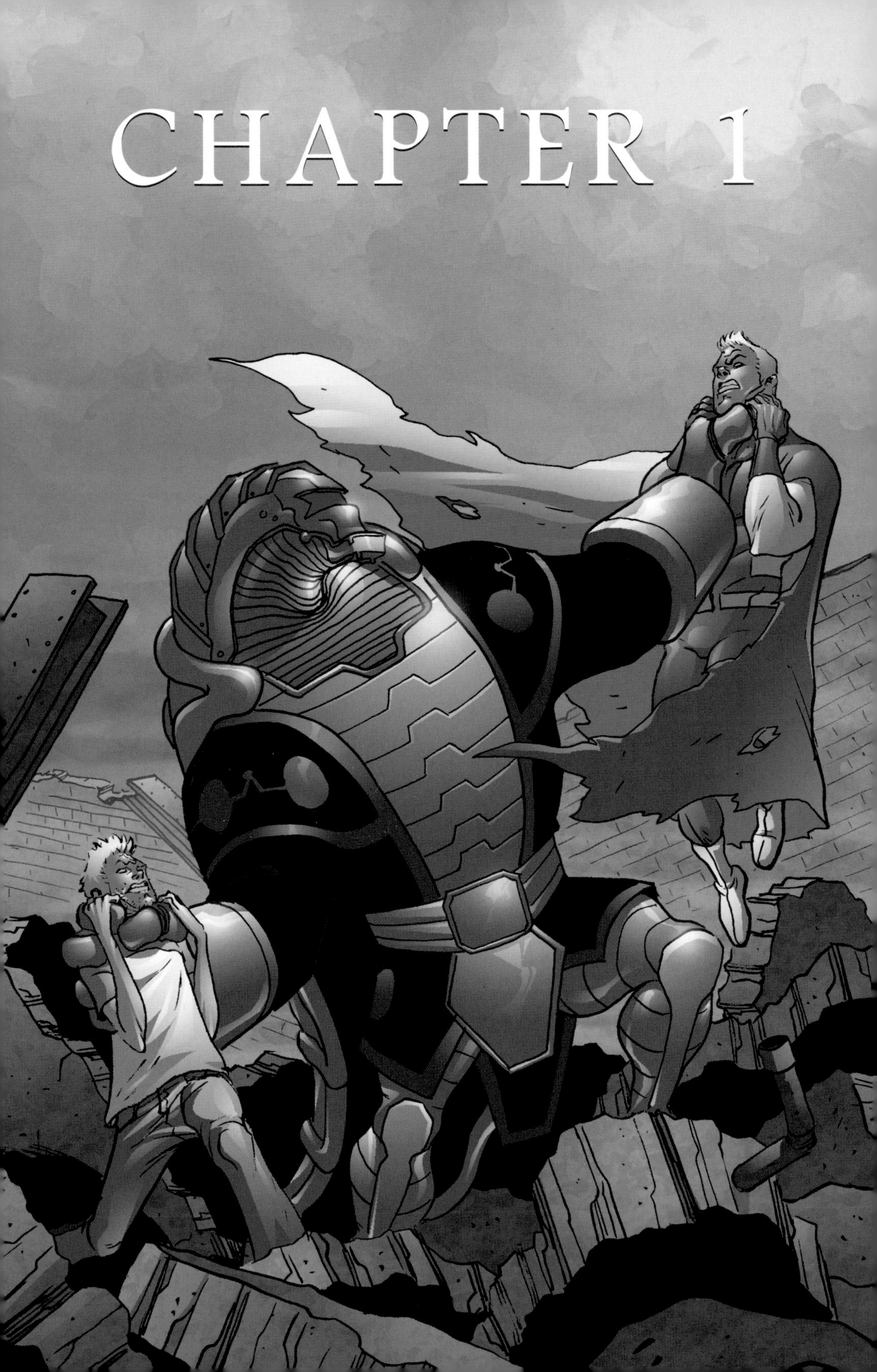

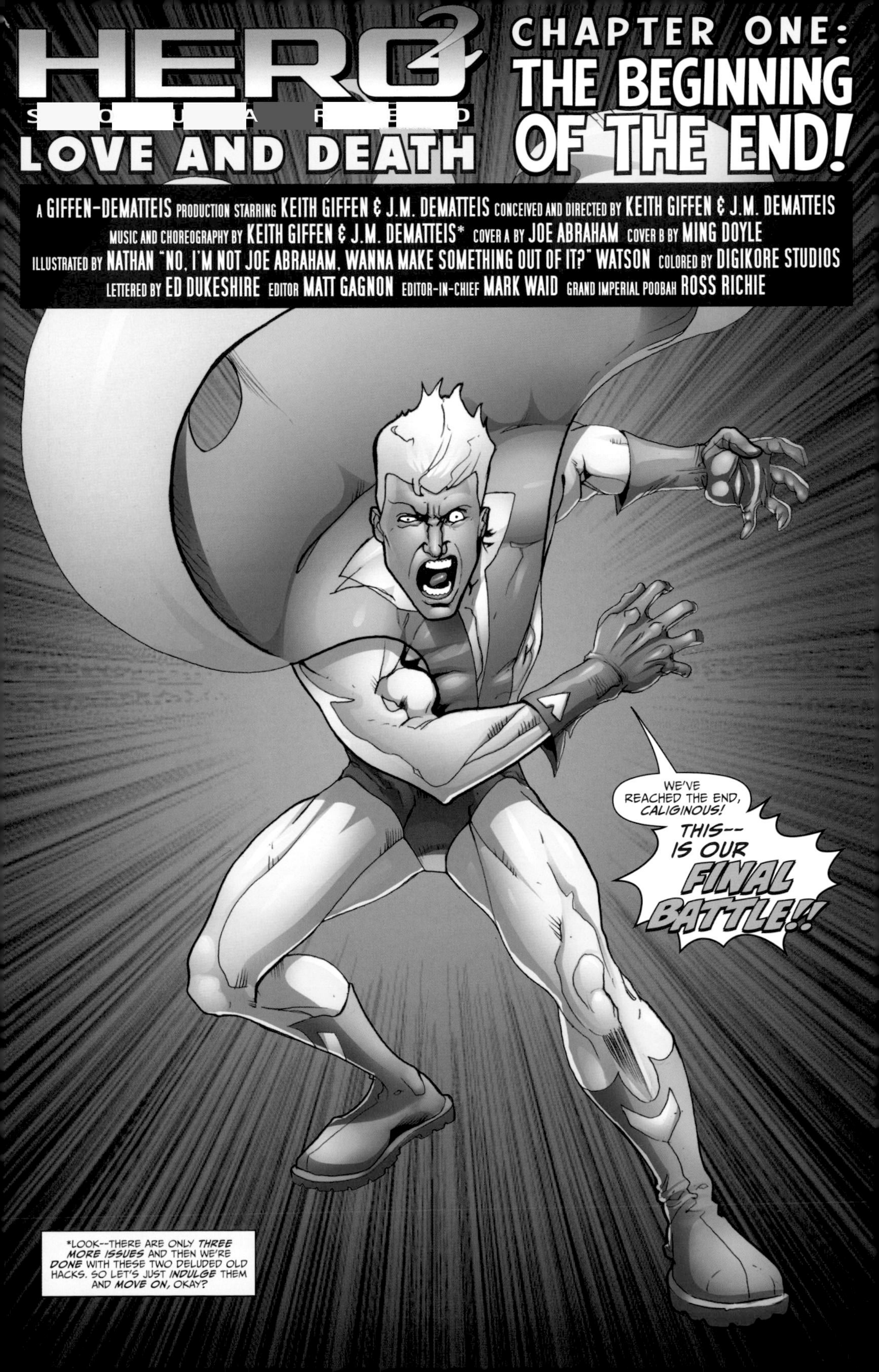
HERO² SQUARED
LOVE AND DEATH
CHAPTER ONE:
THE BEGINNING OF THE END!
A GIFFEN-DEMATTEIS PRODUCTION STARRING KEITH GIFFEN & J.M. DEMATTEIS CONCEIVED AND DIRECTED BY KEITH GIFFEN & J.M. DEMATTEIS
MUSIC AND CHOREOGRAPHY BY KEITH GIFFEN & J.M. DEMATTEIS* COVER A BY JOE ABRAHAM COVER B BY MING DOYLE
ILLUSTRATED BY NATHAN "NO, I'M NOT JOE ABRAHAM, WANNA MAKE SOMETHING OUT OF IT?" WATSON COLORED BY DIGIKORE STUDIOS
LETTERED BY ED DUKESHIRE EDITOR MATT GAGNON EDITOR-IN-CHIEF MARK WAID GRAND IMPERIAL POOBAH ROSS RICHIE
WE'VE REACHED THE END, CALIGINOUS! THIS-- IS OUR FINAL BATTLE!!
*LOOK--THERE ARE ONLY THREE MORE ISSUES AND THEN WE'RE DONE WITH THESE TWO DELUDED OLD HACKS. SO LET'S JUST INDULGE THEM AND MOVE ON, OKAY?

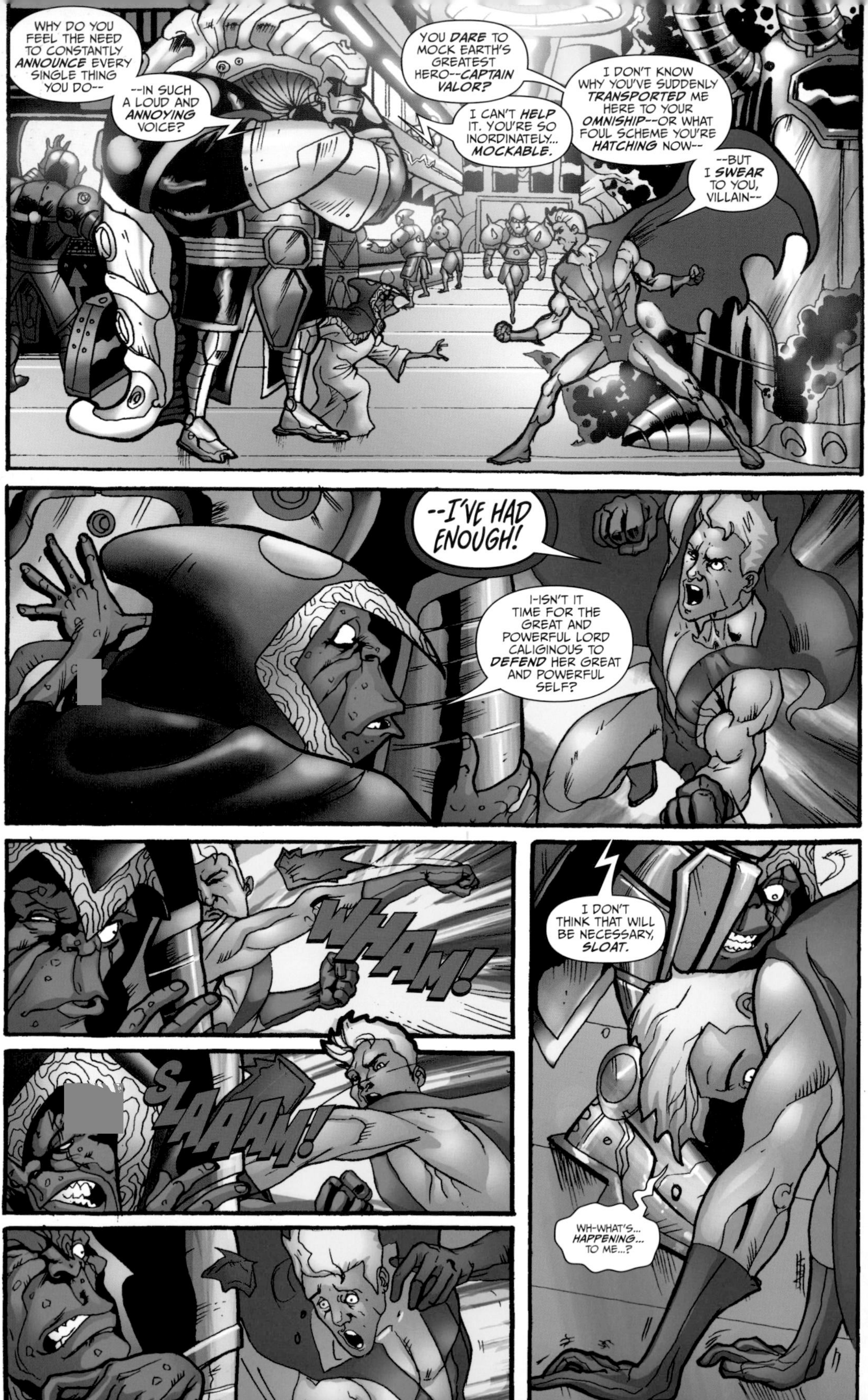
WHY DO YOU FEEL THE NEED TO CONSTANTLY ANNOUNCE EVERY SINGLE THING YOU DO--
--IN SUCH A LOUD AND ANNOYING VOICE?
YOU DARE TO MOCK EARTH'S GREATEST HERO--CAPTAIN VALOR?
I CAN'T HELP IT. YOU'RE SO INORDINATELY... MOCKABLE.
I DON'T KNOW WHY YOU'VE SUDDENLY TRANSPORTED ME HERE TO YOUR OMNISHIP--OR WHAT FOUL SCHEME YOU'RE HATCHING NOW--
--BUT I SWEAR TO YOU, VILLAIN--
--I'VE HAD ENOUGH!
I-ISN'T IT TIME FOR THE GREAT AND POWERFUL LORD CALIGINOUS TO DEFEND HER GREAT AND POWERFUL SELF?
WHAM!
SLAAAM!
I DON'T THINK THAT WILL BE NECESSARY, SLOAT.
WH-WHAT'S... HAPPENING... TO ME...?

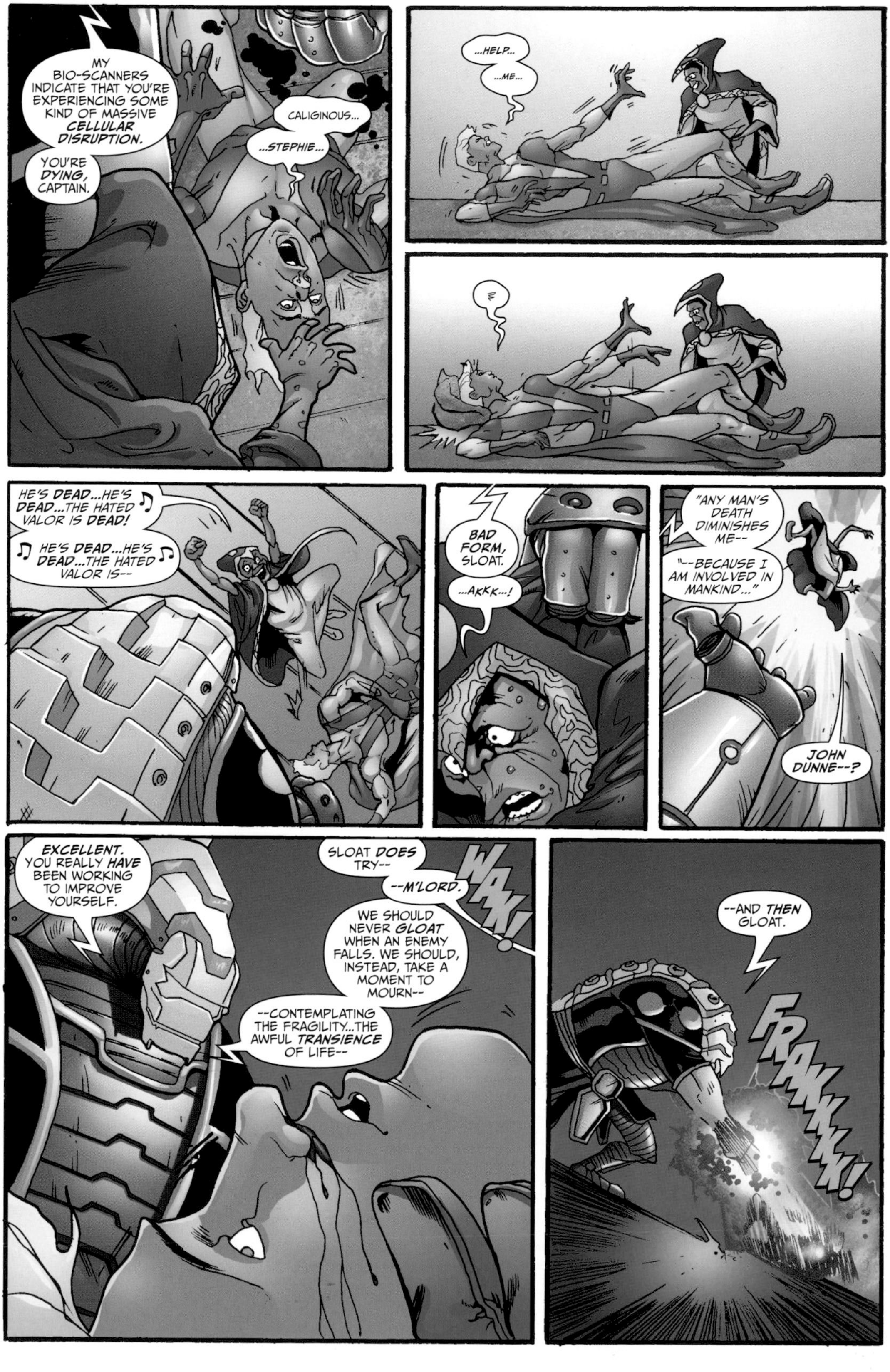
MY BIO-SCANNERS INDICATE THAT YOU'RE EXPERIENCING SOME KIND OF MASSIVE CELLULAR DISRUPTION.
YOU'RE DYING, CAPTAIN.
CALIGINOUS...
...STEPHIE...
...HELP...
...ME...
HE'S DEAD...HE'S DEAD...THE HATED VALOR IS DEAD!
HE'S DEAD...HE'S DEAD...THE HATED VALOR IS--
BAD FORM, SLOAT.
...AKKK...!
"ANY MAN'S DEATH DIMINISHES ME--
"--BECAUSE I AM INVOLVED IN MANKIND..."
JOHN DUNNE--?
EXCELLENT. YOU REALLY HAVE BEEN WORKING TO IMPROVE YOURSELF.
SLOAT DOES TRY--
--M'LORD.
WAK!
WE SHOULD NEVER GLOAT WHEN AN ENEMY FALLS. WE SHOULD, INSTEAD, TAKE A MOMENT TO MOURN--
--CONTEMPLATING THE FRAGILITY...THE AWFUL TRANSIENCE OF LIFE--
--AND THEN GLOAT.
FRAKKKK!

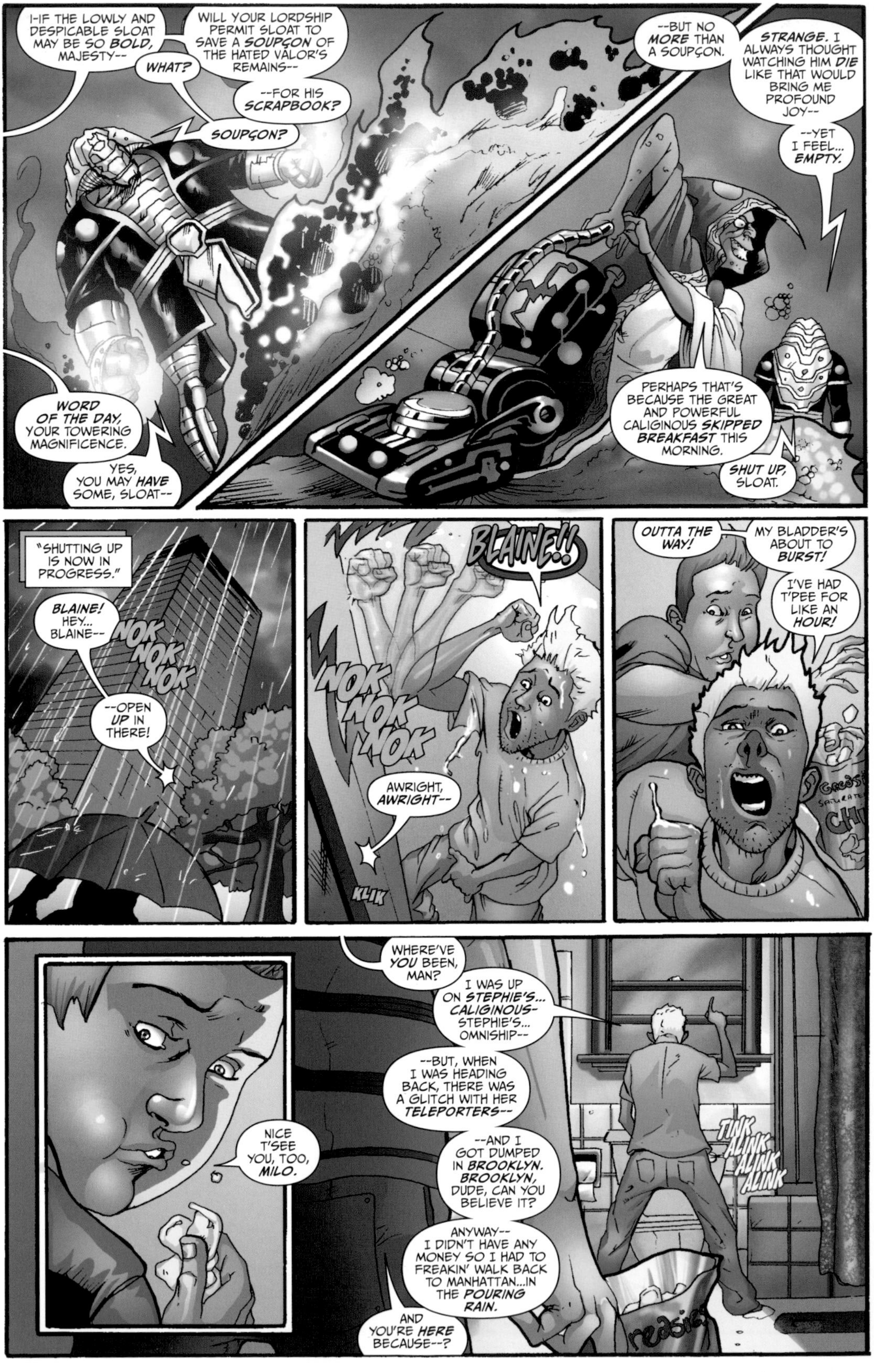
I-IF THE LOWLY AND DESPICABLE SLOAT MAY BE SO BOLD, MAJESTY--
WILL YOUR LORDSHIP PERMIT SLOAT TO SAVE A SOUPÇON OF THE HATED VALOR'S REMAINS--
WHAT?
--FOR HIS SCRAPBOOK?
SOUPÇON?
WORD OF THE DAY, YOUR TOWERING MAGNIFICENCE.
YES, YOU MAY HAVE SOME, SLOAT--
--BUT NO MORE THAN A SOUPÇON.
STRANGE. I ALWAYS THOUGHT WATCHING HIM DIE LIKE THAT WOULD BRING ME PROFOUND JOY--
--YET I FEEL... EMPTY.
PERHAPS THAT'S BECAUSE THE GREAT AND POWERFUL CALIGINOUS SKIPPED BREAKFAST THIS MORNING.
SHUT UP, SLOAT.
"SHUTTING UP IS NOW IN PROGRESS."
BLAINE! HEY... BLAINE--
NOK NOK NOK
--OPEN UP IN THERE!
BLAINE!!
NOK NOK NOK
AWRIGHT, AWRIGHT--
KLIK
OUTTA THE WAY!
MY BLADDER'S ABOUT TO BURST!
I'VE HAD T'PEE FOR LIKE AN HOUR!
WHERE'VE YOU BEEN, MAN?
I WAS UP ON STEPHIE'S... CALIGINOUS-STEPHIE'S... OMNISHIP--
--BUT, WHEN I WAS HEADING BACK, THERE WAS A GLITCH WITH HER TELEPORTERS--
NICE T'SEE YOU, TOO, MILO.
--AND I GOT DUMPED IN BROOKLYN. BROOKLYN, DUDE, CAN YOU BELIEVE IT?
TINK ALINK ALINK ALINK
ANYWAY-- I DIDN'T HAVE ANY MONEY SO I HAD TO FREAKIN' WALK BACK TO MANHATTAN...IN THE POURING RAIN.
AND YOU'RE HERE BECAUSE--?

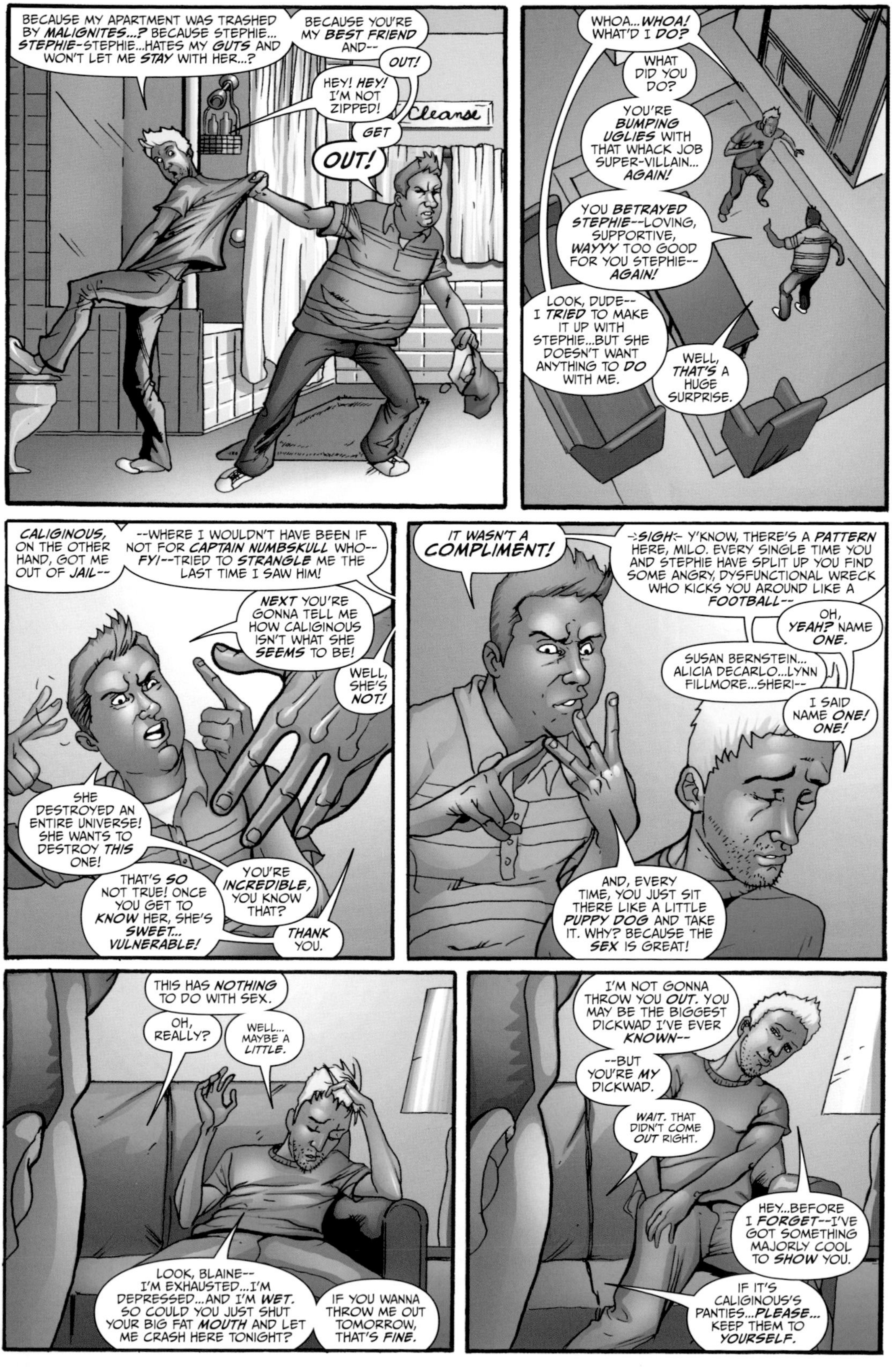

BECAUSE MY APARTMENT WAS TRASHED BY MALIGNITES...? BECAUSE STEPHIE... STEPHIE-STEPHIE...HATES MY GUTS AND WON'T LET ME STAY WITH HER...?
BECAUSE YOU'RE MY BEST FRIEND AND--
OUT!
HEY! HEY! I'M NOT ZIPPED!
GET
OUT!
Cleanse
WHOA...WHOA! WHAT'D I DO?
WHAT DID YOU DO?
YOU'RE BUMPING UGLIES WITH THAT WHACK JOB SUPER-VILLAIN... AGAIN!
YOU BETRAYED STEPHIE--LOVING, SUPPORTIVE, WAYYY TOO GOOD FOR YOU STEPHIE-- AGAIN!
LOOK, DUDE-- I TRIED TO MAKE IT UP WITH STEPHIE...BUT SHE DOESN'T WANT ANYTHING TO DO WITH ME.
WELL, THAT'S A HUGE SURPRISE.
CALIGINOUS, ON THE OTHER HAND, GOT ME OUT OF JAIL--
--WHERE I WOULDN'T HAVE BEEN IF NOT FOR CAPTAIN NUMBSKULL WHO-- FYI--TRIED TO STRANGLE ME THE LAST TIME I SAW HIM!
NEXT YOU'RE GONNA TELL ME HOW CALIGINOUS ISN'T WHAT SHE SEEMS TO BE!
WELL, SHE'S NOT!
SHE DESTROYED AN ENTIRE UNIVERSE! SHE WANTS TO DESTROY THIS ONE!
THAT'S SO NOT TRUE! ONCE YOU GET TO KNOW HER, SHE'S SWEET... VULNERABLE!
YOU'RE INCREDIBLE, YOU KNOW THAT?
THANK YOU.
IT WASN'T A COMPLIMENT!
-SIGH- Y'KNOW, THERE'S A PATTERN HERE, MILO. EVERY SINGLE TIME YOU AND STEPHIE HAVE SPLIT UP YOU FIND SOME ANGRY, DYSFUNCTIONAL WRECK WHO KICKS YOU AROUND LIKE A FOOTBALL--
OH, YEAH? NAME ONE.
SUSAN BERNSTEIN... ALICIA DECARLO...LYNN FILLMORE...SHERI--
I SAID NAME ONE! ONE!
AND, EVERY TIME, YOU JUST SIT THERE LIKE A LITTLE PUPPY DOG AND TAKE IT. WHY? BECAUSE THE SEX IS GREAT!
THIS HAS NOTHING TO DO WITH SEX.
OH, REALLY?
WELL... MAYBE A LITTLE.
LOOK, BLAINE-- I'M EXHAUSTED...I'M DEPRESSED...AND I'M WET. SO COULD YOU JUST SHUT YOUR BIG FAT MOUTH AND LET ME CRASH HERE TONIGHT?
IF YOU WANNA THROW ME OUT TOMORROW, THAT'S FINE.
I'M NOT GONNA THROW YOU OUT. YOU MAY BE THE BIGGEST DICKWAD I'VE EVER KNOWN--
--BUT YOU'RE MY DICKWAD.
WAIT. THAT DIDN'T COME OUT RIGHT.
HEY...BEFORE I FORGET--I'VE GOT SOMETHING MAJORLY COOL TO SHOW YOU.
IF IT'S CALIGINOUS'S PANTIES...PLEASE... KEEP THEM TO YOURSELF.

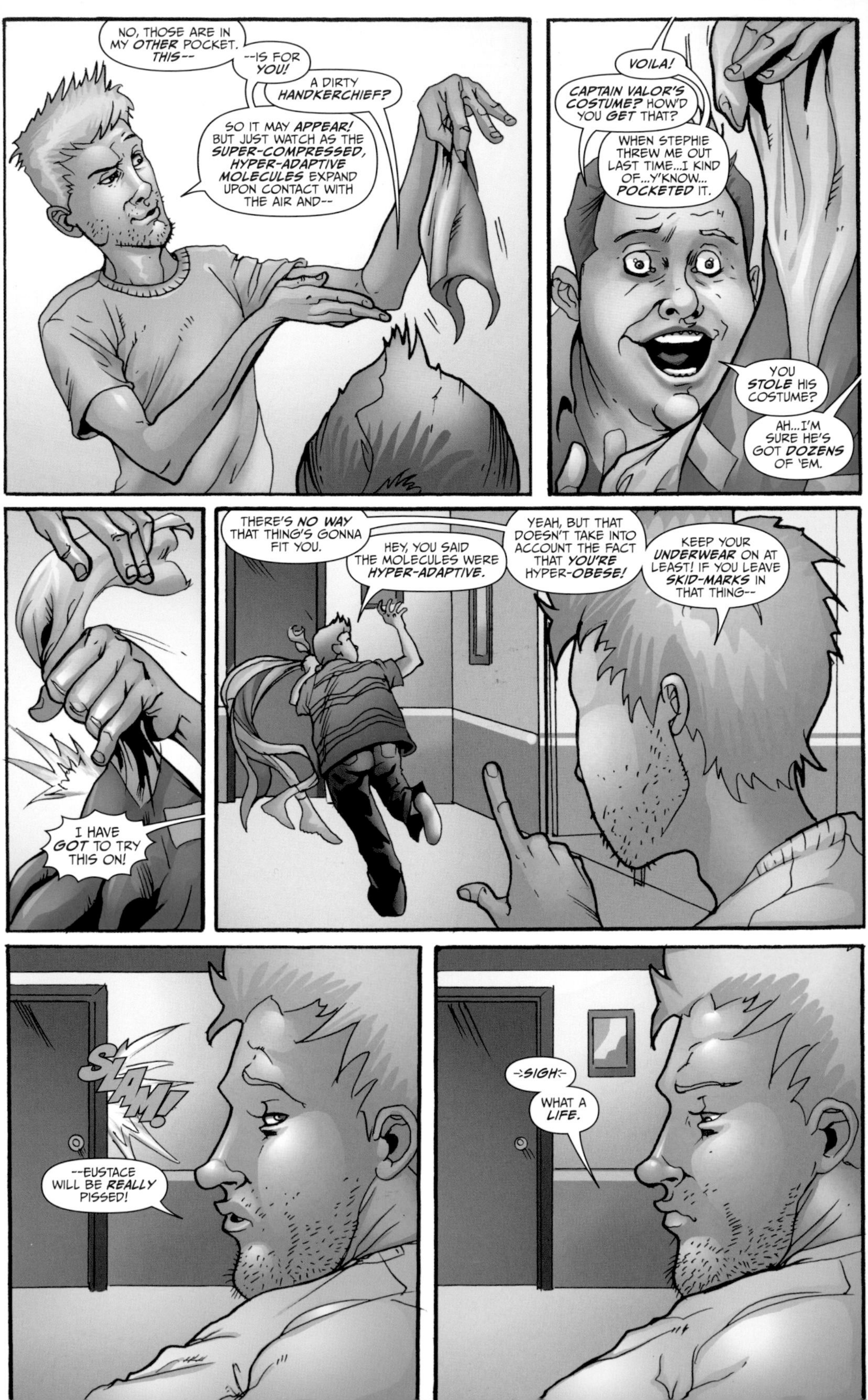
NO, THOSE ARE IN MY OTHER POCKET. THIS--
--IS FOR YOU!
A DIRTY HANDKERCHIEF?
SO IT MAY APPEAR! BUT JUST WATCH AS THE SUPER-COMPRESSED, HYPER-ADAPTIVE MOLECULES EXPAND UPON CONTACT WITH THE AIR AND--
VOILA!
CAPTAIN VALOR'S COSTUME? HOW'D YOU GET THAT?
WHEN STEPHIE THREW ME OUT LAST TIME...I KIND OF...Y'KNOW... POCKETED IT.
YOU STOLE HIS COSTUME?
AH...I'M SURE HE'S GOT DOZENS OF 'EM.
I HAVE GOT TO TRY THIS ON!
THERE'S NO WAY THAT THING'S GONNA FIT YOU.
HEY, YOU SAID THE MOLECULES WERE HYPER-ADAPTIVE.
YEAH, BUT THAT DOESN'T TAKE INTO ACCOUNT THE FACT THAT YOU'RE HYPER-OBESE!
KEEP YOUR UNDERWEAR ON AT LEAST! IF YOU LEAVE SKID-MARKS IN THAT THING--
SLAM!
--EUSTACE WILL BE REALLY PISSED!
-SIGH-
WHAT A LIFE.

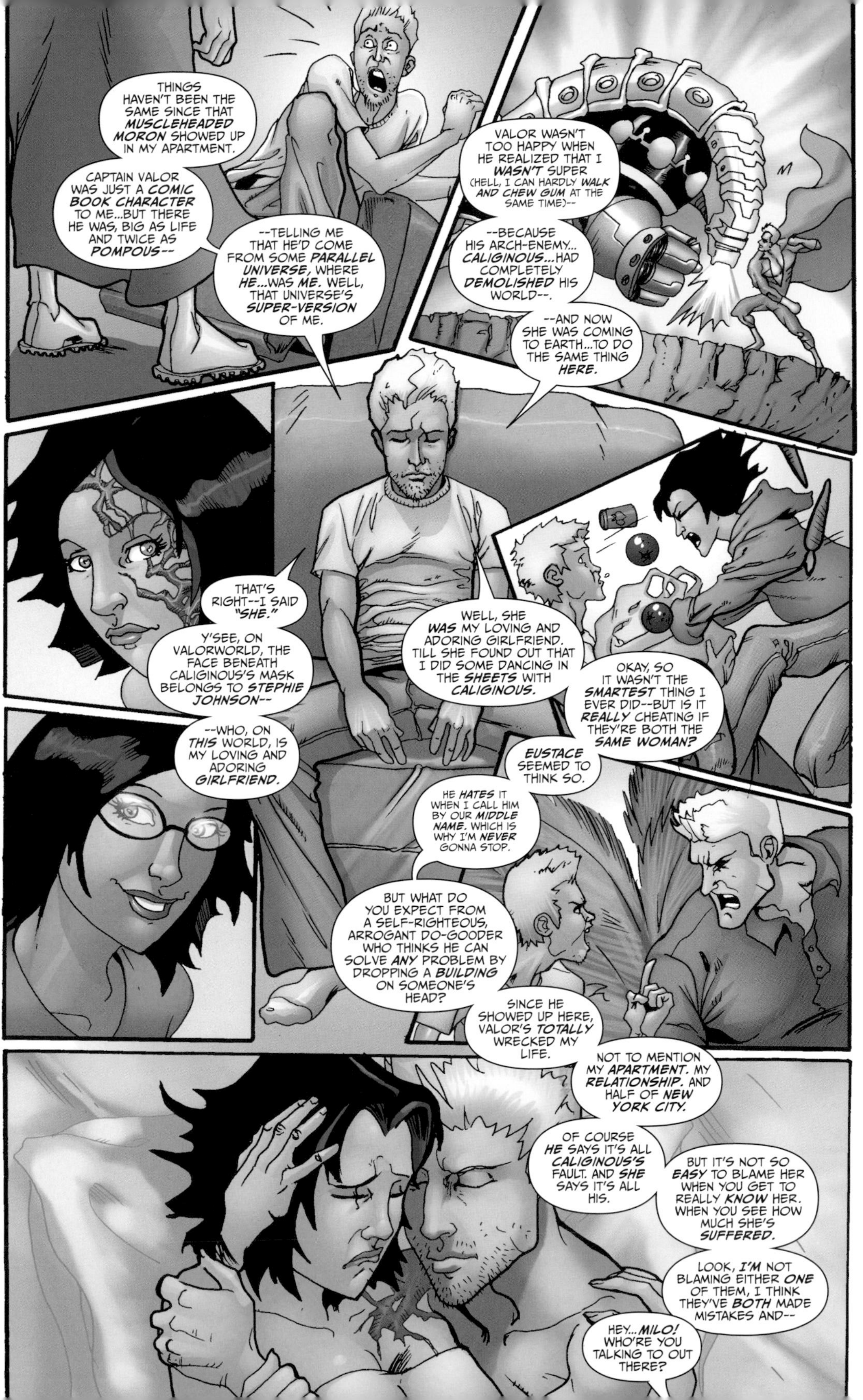
THINGS HAVEN'T BEEN THE SAME SINCE THAT MUSCLEHEADED MORON SHOWED UP IN MY APARTMENT.
CAPTAIN VALOR WAS JUST A COMIC BOOK CHARACTER TO ME...BUT THERE HE WAS, BIG AS LIFE AND TWICE AS POMPOUS--
--TELLING ME THAT HE'D COME FROM SOME PARALLEL UNIVERSE, WHERE HE...WAS ME. WELL, THAT UNIVERSE'S SUPER-VERSION OF ME.
VALOR WASN'T TOO HAPPY WHEN HE REALIZED THAT I WASN'T SUPER (HELL, I CAN HARDLY WALK AND CHEW GUM AT THE SAME TIME)--
--BECAUSE HIS ARCH-ENEMY... CALIGINOUS...HAD COMPLETELY DEMOLISHED HIS WORLD--.
--AND NOW SHE WAS COMING TO EARTH...TO DO THE SAME THING HERE.
THAT'S RIGHT--I SAID "SHE."
Y'SEE, ON VALORWORLD, THE FACE BENEATH CALIGINOUS'S MASK BELONGS TO STEPHIE JOHNSON--
--WHO, ON THIS WORLD, IS MY LOVING AND ADORING GIRLFRIEND.
WELL, SHE WAS MY LOVING AND ADORING GIRLFRIEND. TILL SHE FOUND OUT THAT I DID SOME DANCING IN THE SHEETS WITH CALIGINOUS.
OKAY, SO IT WASN'T THE SMARTEST THING I EVER DID--BUT IS IT REALLY CHEATING IF THEY'RE BOTH THE SAME WOMAN?
EUSTACE SEEMED TO THINK SO.
HE HATES IT WHEN I CALL HIM BY OUR MIDDLE NAME. WHICH IS WHY I'M NEVER GONNA STOP.
BUT WHAT DO YOU EXPECT FROM A SELF-RIGHTEOUS, ARROGANT DO-GOODER WHO THINKS HE CAN SOLVE ANY PROBLEM BY DROPPING A BUILDING ON SOMEONE'S HEAD?
SINCE HE SHOWED UP HERE, VALOR'S TOTALLY WRECKED MY LIFE.
NOT TO MENTION MY APARTMENT. MY RELATIONSHIP. AND HALF OF NEW YORK CITY.
OF COURSE HE SAYS IT'S ALL CALIGINOUS'S FAULT. AND SHE SAYS IT'S ALL HIS.
BUT IT'S NOT SO EASY TO BLAME HER WHEN YOU GET TO REALLY KNOW HER. WHEN YOU SEE HOW MUCH SHE'S SUFFERED.
LOOK, I'M NOT BLAMING EITHER ONE OF THEM, I THINK THEY'VE BOTH MADE MISTAKES AND--
HEY...MILO! WHO'RE YOU TALKING TO OUT THERE?

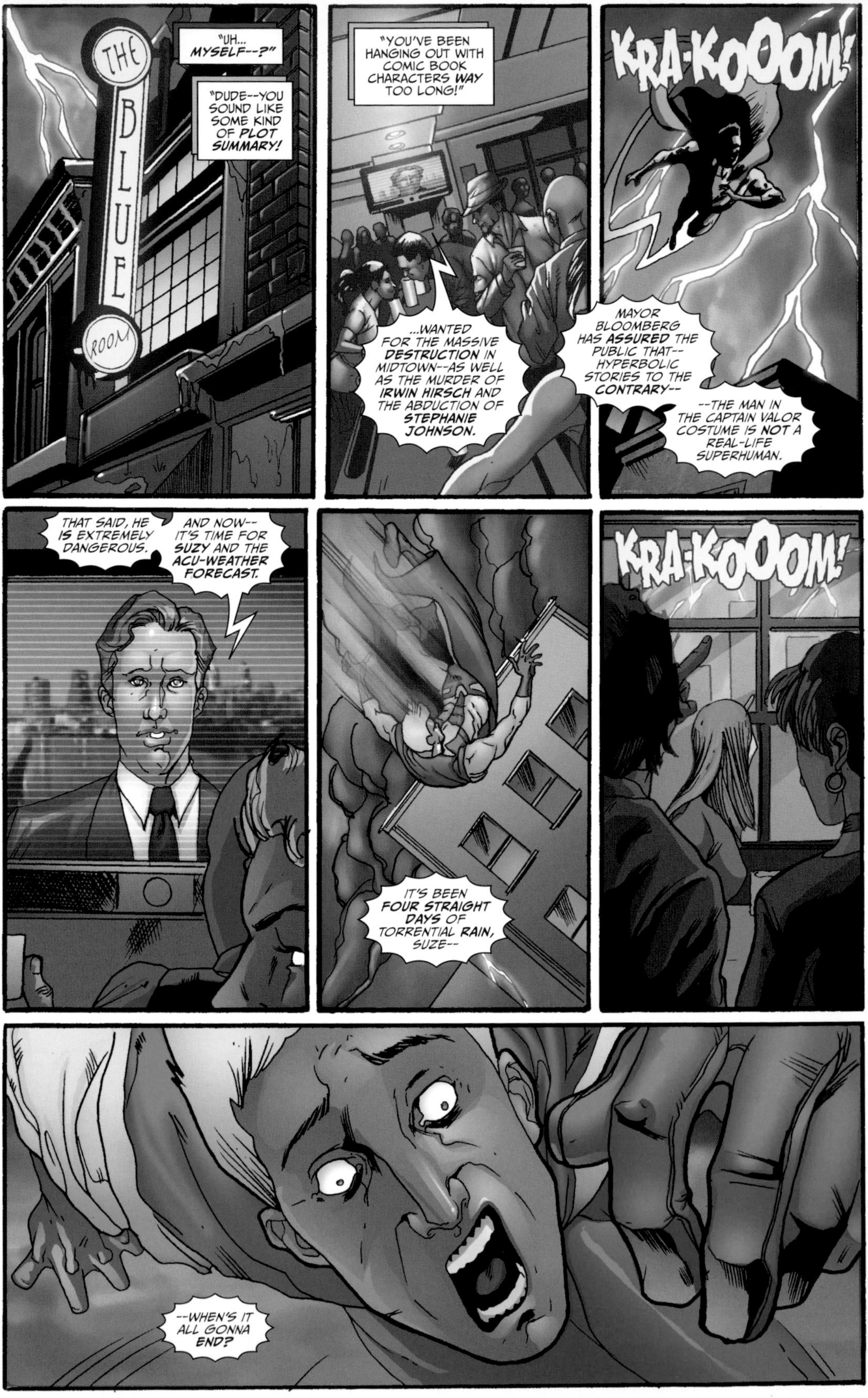
THE BLUE ROOM
"UH... MYSELF--?"
"DUDE--YOU SOUND LIKE SOME KIND OF PLOT SUMMARY!
"YOU'VE BEEN HANGING OUT WITH COMIC BOOK CHARACTERS WAY TOO LONG!"
...WANTED FOR THE MASSIVE DESTRUCTION IN MIDTOWN--AS WELL AS THE MURDER OF IRWIN HIRSCH AND THE ABDUCTION OF STEPHANIE JOHNSON.
KRA-KOOOM!
MAYOR BLOOMBERG HAS ASSURED THE PUBLIC THAT--HYPERBOLIC STORIES TO THE CONTRARY--
--THE MAN IN THE CAPTAIN VALOR COSTUME IS NOT A REAL-LIFE SUPERHUMAN.
THAT SAID, HE IS EXTREMELY DANGEROUS.
AND NOW--IT'S TIME FOR SUZY AND THE ACU-WEATHER FORECAST.
IT'S BEEN FOUR STRAIGHT DAYS OF TORRENTIAL RAIN, SUZE--
KRA-KOOOM!
--WHEN'S IT ALL GONNA END?

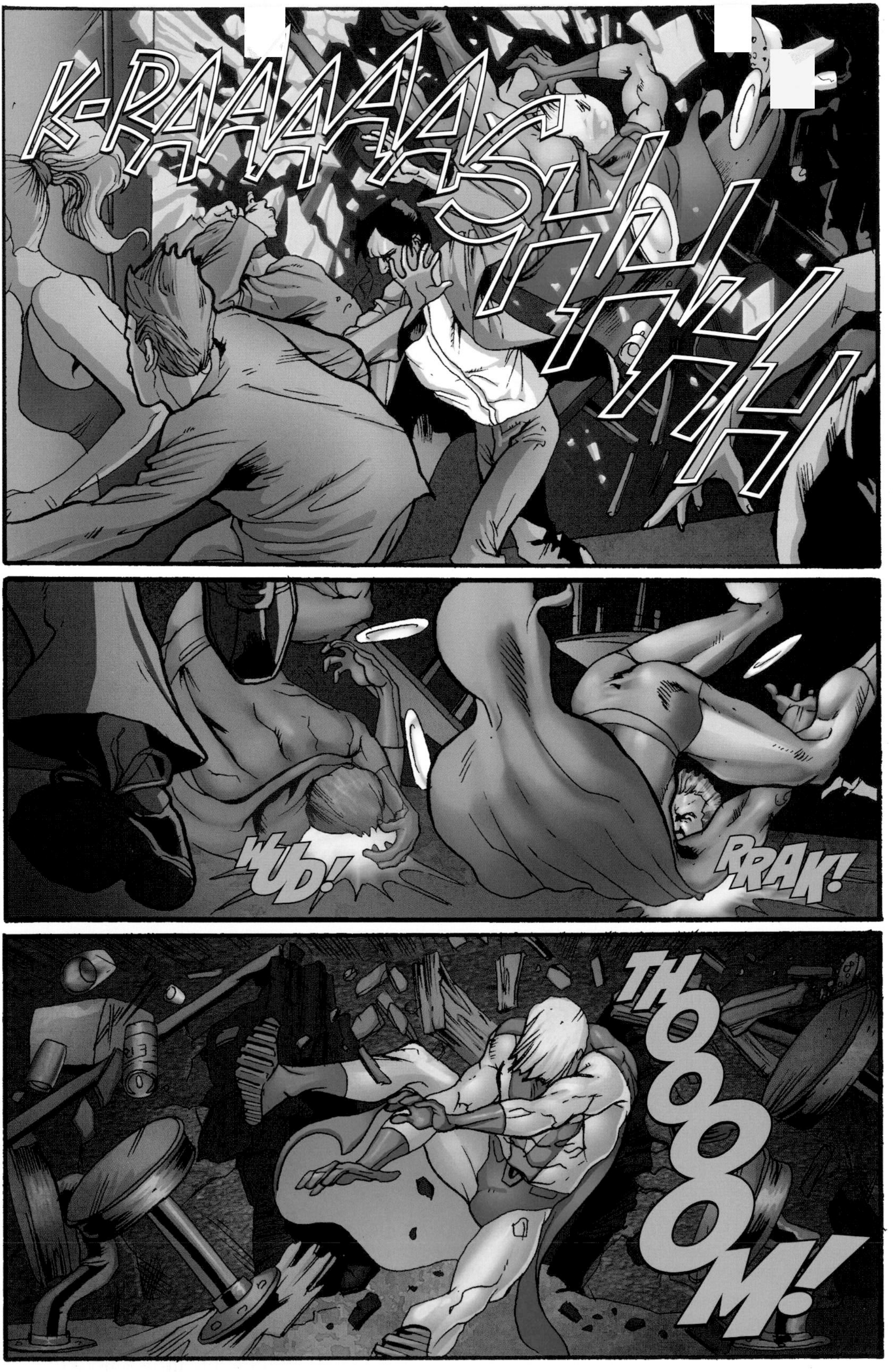
K-RAAAAAASHHHH
WUD!
RRAK!
THOOOOM!

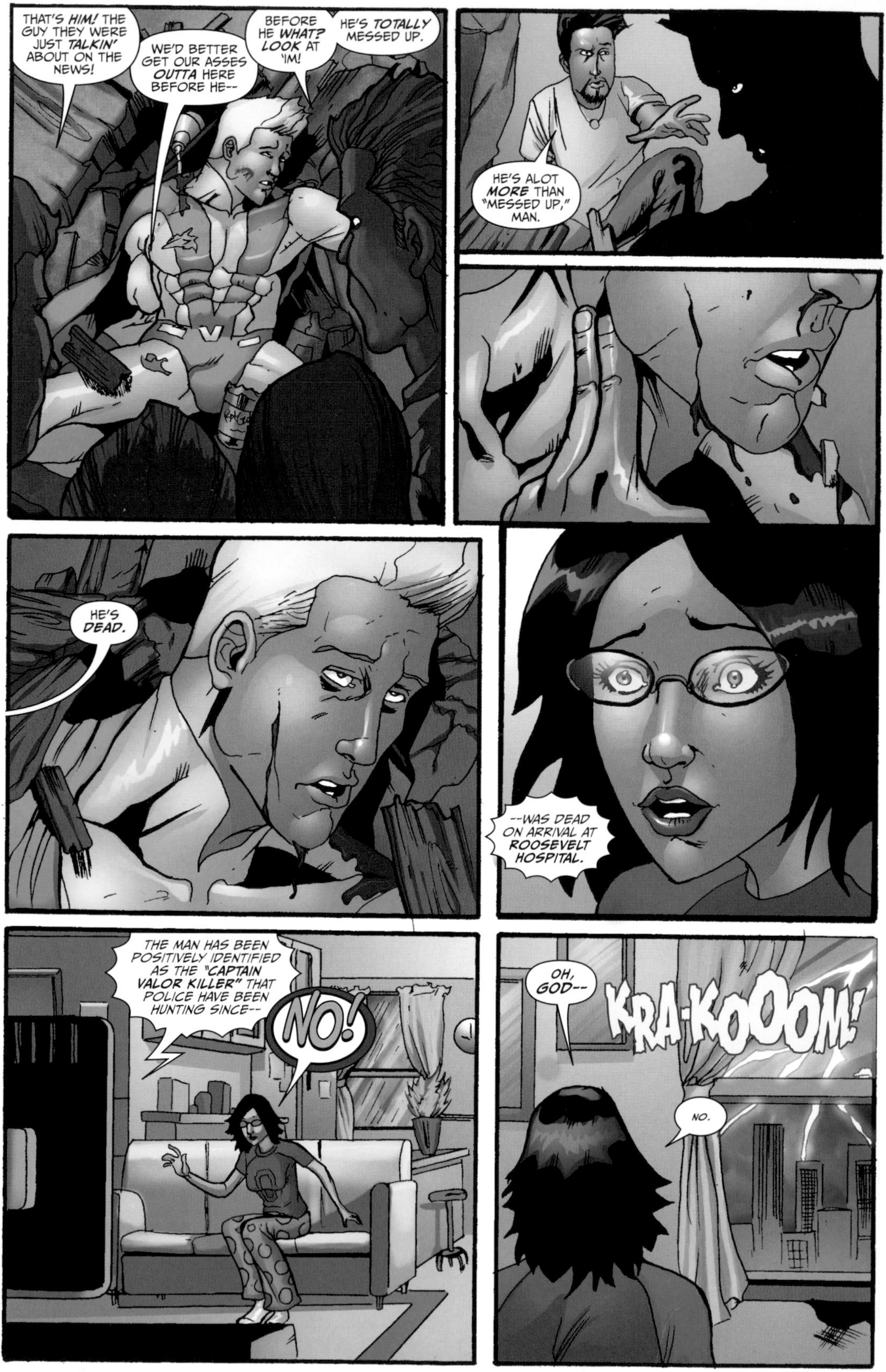

THAT'S HIM! THE GUY THEY WERE JUST TALKIN' ABOUT ON THE NEWS!
WE'D BETTER GET OUR ASSES OUTTA HERE BEFORE HE--
BEFORE HE WHAT? LOOK AT 'IM!
HE'S TOTALLY MESSED UP.
HE'S ALOT MORE THAN "MESSED UP," MAN.
HE'S DEAD.
--WAS DEAD ON ARRIVAL AT ROOSEVELT HOSPITAL.
THE MAN HAS BEEN POSITIVELY IDENTIFIED AS THE "CAPTAIN VALOR KILLER" THAT POLICE HAVE BEEN HUNTING SINCE--
NO!
OH, GOD--
KRA-KOOOM!
NO.

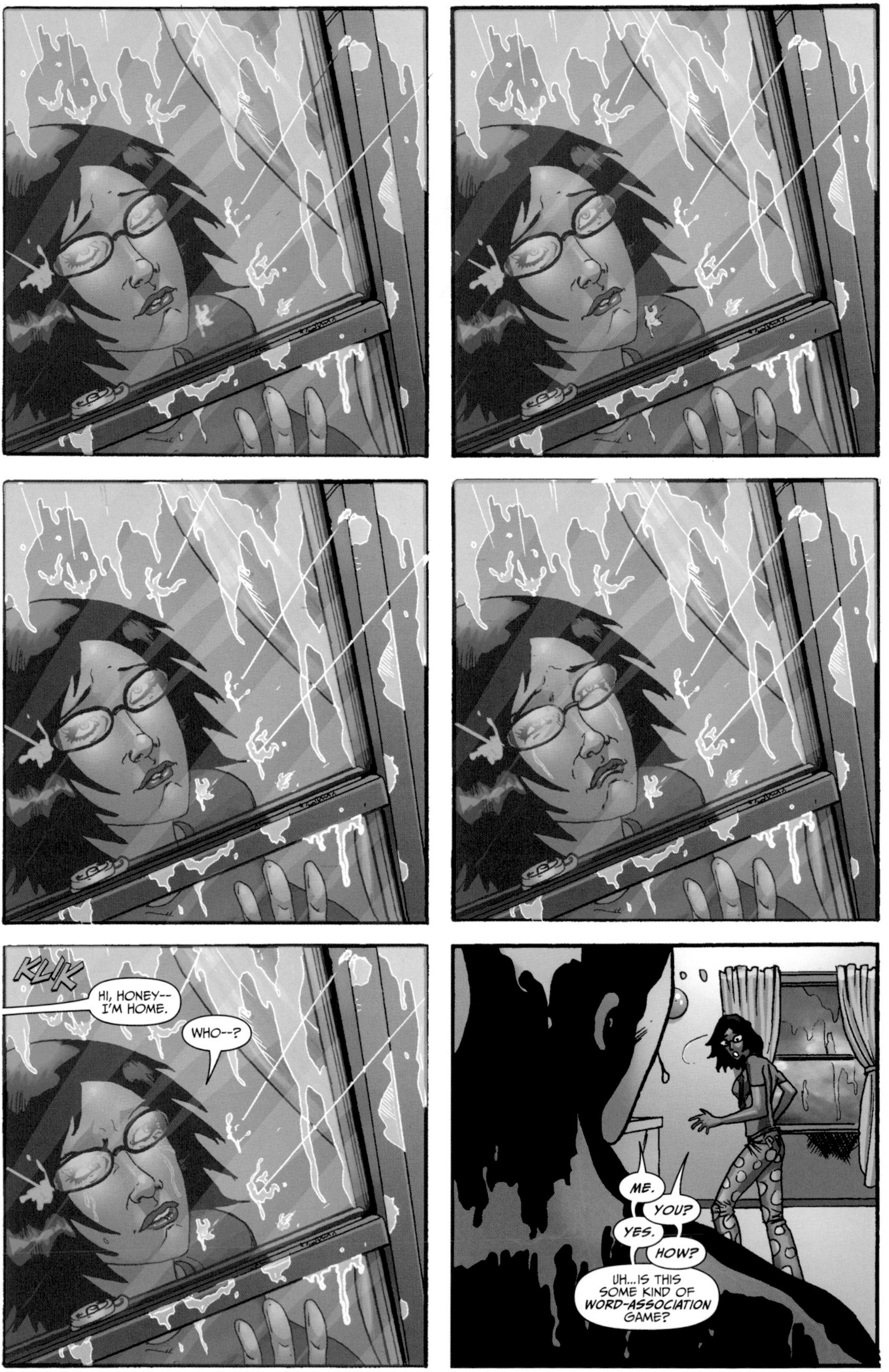
KLIK
HI, HONEY-- I'M HOME.
WHO--?
ME.
YOU?
YES.
HOW?
UH...IS THIS SOME KIND OF WORD-ASSOCIATION GAME?

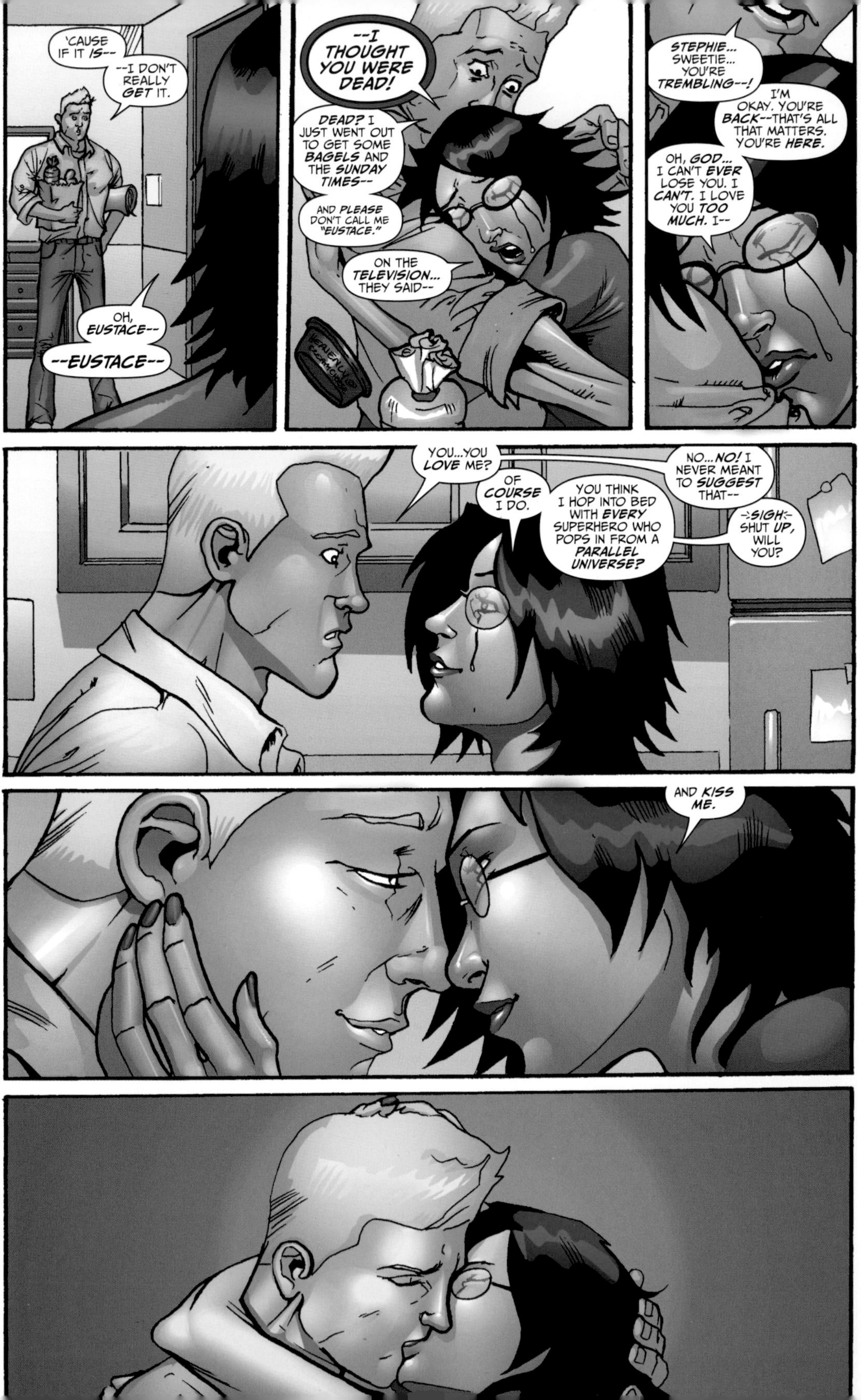

'CAUSE IF IT *IS*--
--I DON'T REALLY *GET* IT.
OH, *EUSTACE*--
--EUSTACE--
--I THOUGHT YOU WERE DEAD!
DEAD? I JUST WENT OUT TO GET SOME *BAGELS* AND THE *SUNDAY TIMES*--
AND *PLEASE* DON'T CALL ME *"EUSTACE."*
ON THE *TELEVISION*... THEY SAID--
STEPHIE... SWEETIE... YOU'RE *TREMBLING*--!
I'M OKAY. YOU'RE *BACK*--THAT'S ALL THAT MATTERS. YOU'RE *HERE*.
OH, *GOD*... I CAN'T *EVER* LOSE YOU. I *CAN'T*. I LOVE YOU *TOO MUCH*. I--
YOU...YOU *LOVE* ME?
OF *COURSE* I DO.
YOU THINK I HOP INTO BED WITH *EVERY* SUPERHERO WHO POPS IN FROM A *PARALLEL UNIVERSE?*
NO...*NO!* I NEVER MEANT TO *SUGGEST* THAT--
SIGH SHUT *UP*, WILL YOU?
AND *KISS ME*.

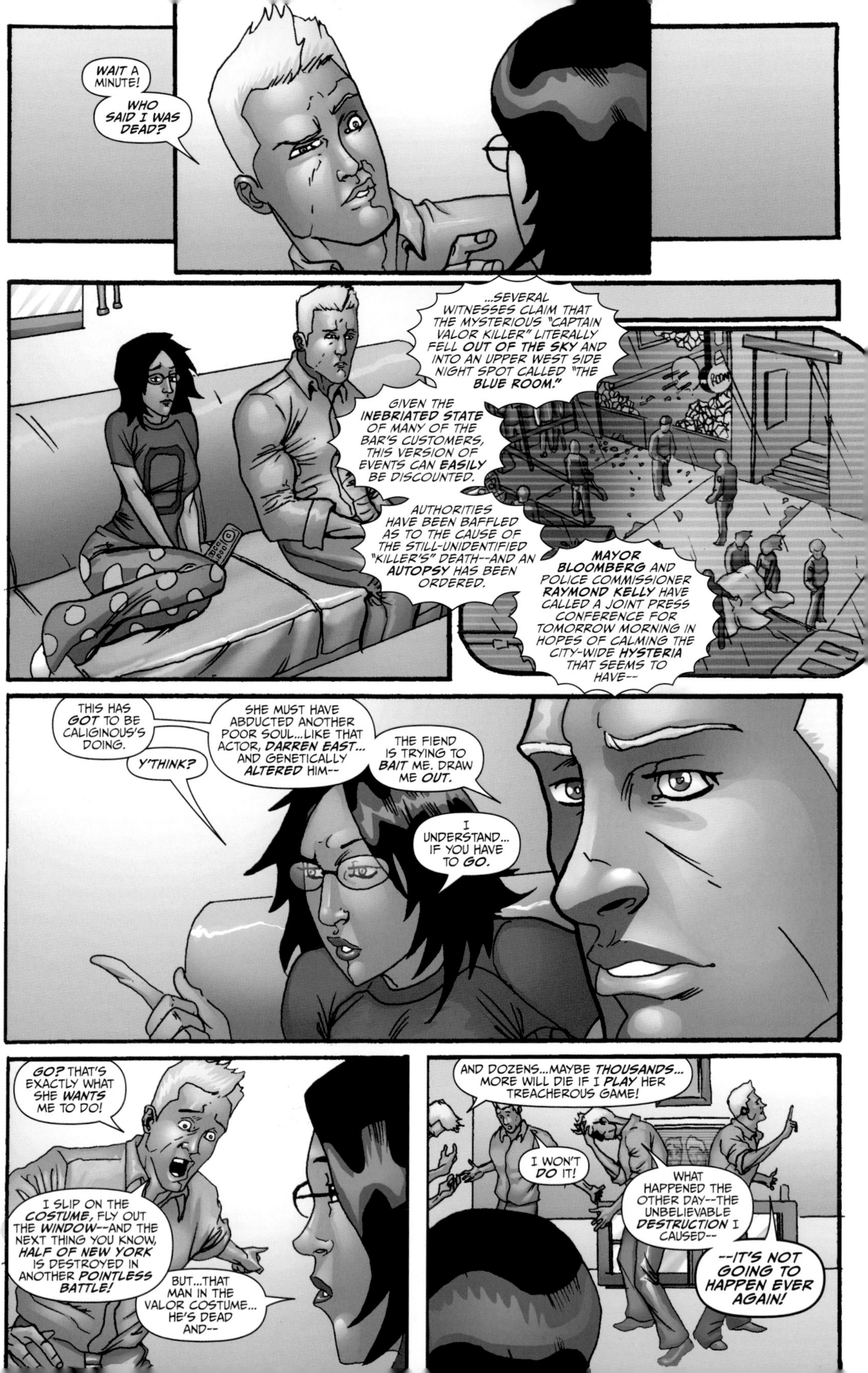
WAIT A MINUTE! WHO SAID I WAS DEAD?
...SEVERAL WITNESSES CLAIM THAT THE MYSTERIOUS "CAPTAIN VALOR KILLER" LITERALLY FELL OUT OF THE SKY AND INTO AN UPPER WEST SIDE NIGHT SPOT CALLED "THE BLUE ROOM."
GIVEN THE INEBRIATED STATE OF MANY OF THE BAR'S CUSTOMERS, THIS VERSION OF EVENTS CAN EASILY BE DISCOUNTED.
AUTHORITIES HAVE BEEN BAFFLED AS TO THE CAUSE OF THE STILL-UNIDENTIFIED "KILLER'S" DEATH--AND AN AUTOPSY HAS BEEN ORDERED.
MAYOR BLOOMBERG AND POLICE COMMISSIONER RAYMOND KELLY HAVE CALLED A JOINT PRESS CONFERENCE FOR TOMORROW MORNING IN HOPES OF CALMING THE CITY-WIDE HYSTERIA THAT SEEMS TO HAVE--
THIS HAS GOT TO BE CALIGINOUS'S DOING.
Y'THINK?
SHE MUST HAVE ABDUCTED ANOTHER POOR SOUL...LIKE THAT ACTOR, DARREN EAST... AND GENETICALLY ALTERED HIM--
THE FIEND IS TRYING TO BAIT ME. DRAW ME OUT.
I UNDERSTAND... IF YOU HAVE TO GO.
GO? THAT'S EXACTLY WHAT SHE WANTS ME TO DO!
I SLIP ON THE COSTUME, FLY OUT THE WINDOW--AND THE NEXT THING YOU KNOW, HALF OF NEW YORK IS DESTROYED IN ANOTHER POINTLESS BATTLE!
BUT...THAT MAN IN THE VALOR COSTUME... HE'S DEAD AND--
AND DOZENS...MAYBE THOUSANDS... MORE WILL DIE IF I PLAY HER TREACHEROUS GAME!
I WON'T DO IT!
WHAT HAPPENED THE OTHER DAY--THE UNBELIEVABLE DESTRUCTION I CAUSED--
--IT'S NOT GOING TO HAPPEN EVER AGAIN!

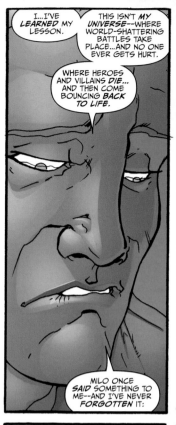

I...I'VE *LEARNED* MY LESSON.

THIS ISN'T *MY UNIVERSE*--WHERE WORLD-SHATTERING BATTLES TAKE PLACE...AND NO ONE EVER GETS HURT.

WHERE HEROES AND VILLAINS *DIE*... AND THEN COME BOUNCING *BACK* TO LIFE.

MILO ONCE *SAID* SOMETHING TO ME--AND I'VE NEVER *FORGOTTEN* IT:

"MAYBE WHERE YOU COME FROM LIFE REALLY *IS* LIKE A COMIC BOOK--BUT HERE IT DOESN'T WORK LIKE THAT.

"WE'VE GOT *ENOUGH* IDIOTS FLYING PLANES INTO BUILDINGS AND DROPPING *BOMBS* ON WOMEN AND BABIES WITHOUT *SOME SELF-RIGHTEOUS SUPER-THUG*--

"--MAKING THINGS EVEN *WORSE*..."

YOU'RE...QUOTING *MILO?*

HE *HAS* BEEN KNOWN TO MAKE SENSE...ON RARE *OCCASIONS.*

BUT YOU CAN'T LET WHAT *HE* SAYS DICTATE HOW YOU'LL--

DO YOU *DISAGREE* WITH HIM?

WHAT?

DO YOU DISAGREE WITH WHAT MILO *SAID?*

I DON'T THINK YOU'RE A "SELF-RIGHTEOUS THUG." I THINK YOU'RE A *HERO.* YOU--

DO YOU *DISAGREE?*

NO.

THEN *THAT'S IT:* CAPTAIN VALOR IS *DEAD.* AND HE'S *NEVER COMING BACK.*

BUT--WHAT ARE YOU GOING TO *DO?* ABOUT CALIGINOUS?

I...I DON'T KNOW.

WE'LL WORK THIS OUT *TOGETHER,* EUSTACE. I *PROMISE* YOU. NOW, C'MON--

--LET'S GO TO BED.

CAN I...AH... JUST SAY *TWO* THINGS?

SURE.

ONE: YOU'RE THE MOST *INCREDIBLE* WOMAN I'VE EVER KNOWN.

AND *TWO...?*

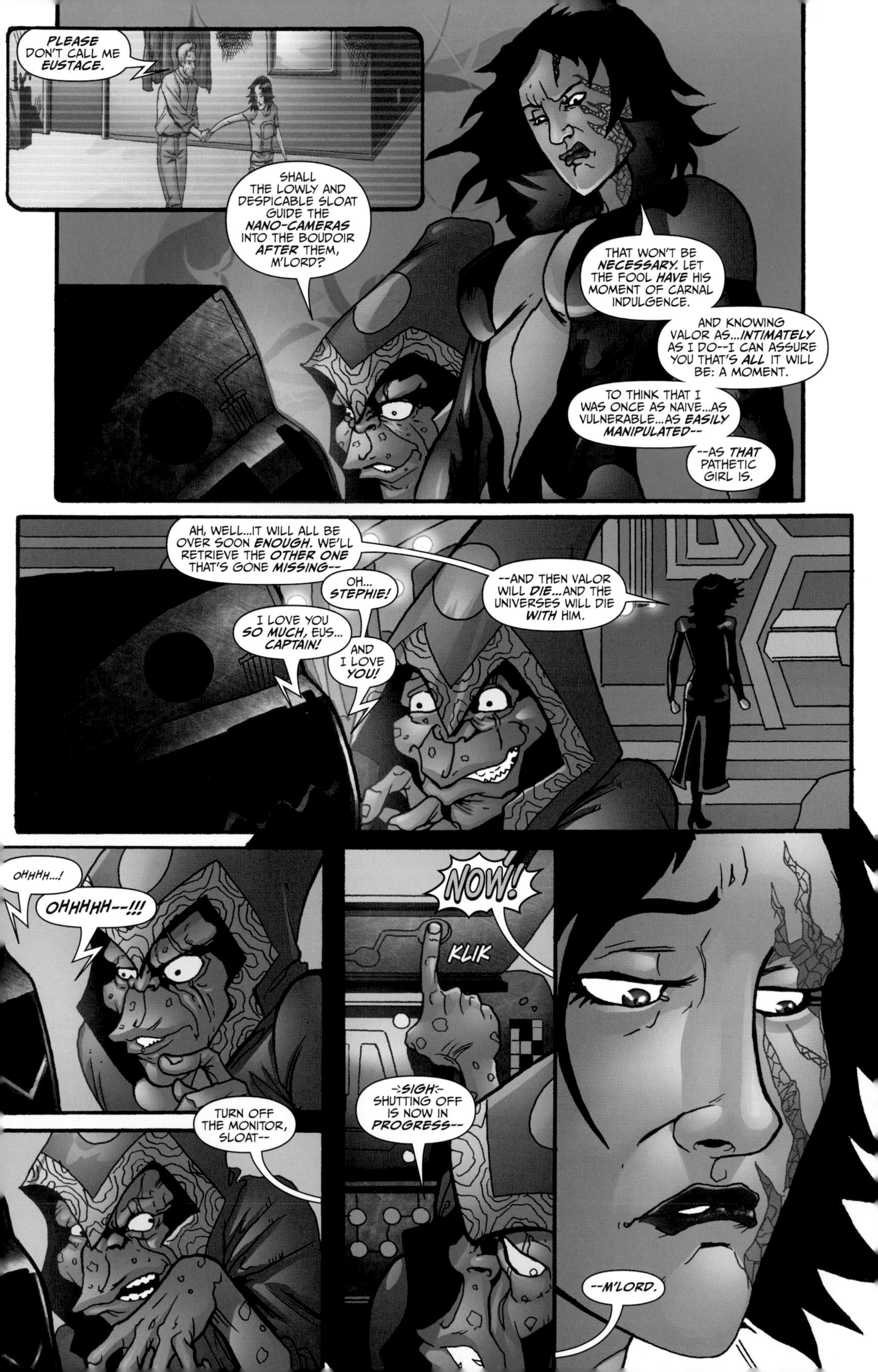
PLEASE DON'T CALL ME EUSTACE.
SHALL THE LOWLY AND DESPICABLE SLOAT GUIDE THE NANO-CAMERAS INTO THE BOUDOIR AFTER THEM, M'LORD?
THAT WON'T BE NECESSARY. LET THE FOOL HAVE HIS MOMENT OF CARNAL INDULGENCE.
AND KNOWING VALOR AS...INTIMATELY AS I DO--I CAN ASSURE YOU THAT'S ALL IT WILL BE: A MOMENT.
TO THINK THAT I WAS ONCE AS NAIVE...AS VULNERABLE...AS EASILY MANIPULATED--
--AS THAT PATHETIC GIRL IS.
AH, WELL...IT WILL ALL BE OVER SOON ENOUGH. WE'LL RETRIEVE THE OTHER ONE THAT'S GONE MISSING--
--AND THEN VALOR WILL DIE...AND THE UNIVERSES WILL DIE WITH HIM.
OH... STEPHIE!
I LOVE YOU SO MUCH, EUS... CAPTAIN!
AND I LOVE YOU!
OHHHH...!
OHHHHH--!!!
NOW!
KLIK
TURN OFF THE MONITOR, SLOAT--
-SIGH- SHUTTING OFF IS NOW IN PROGRESS--
--M'LORD.

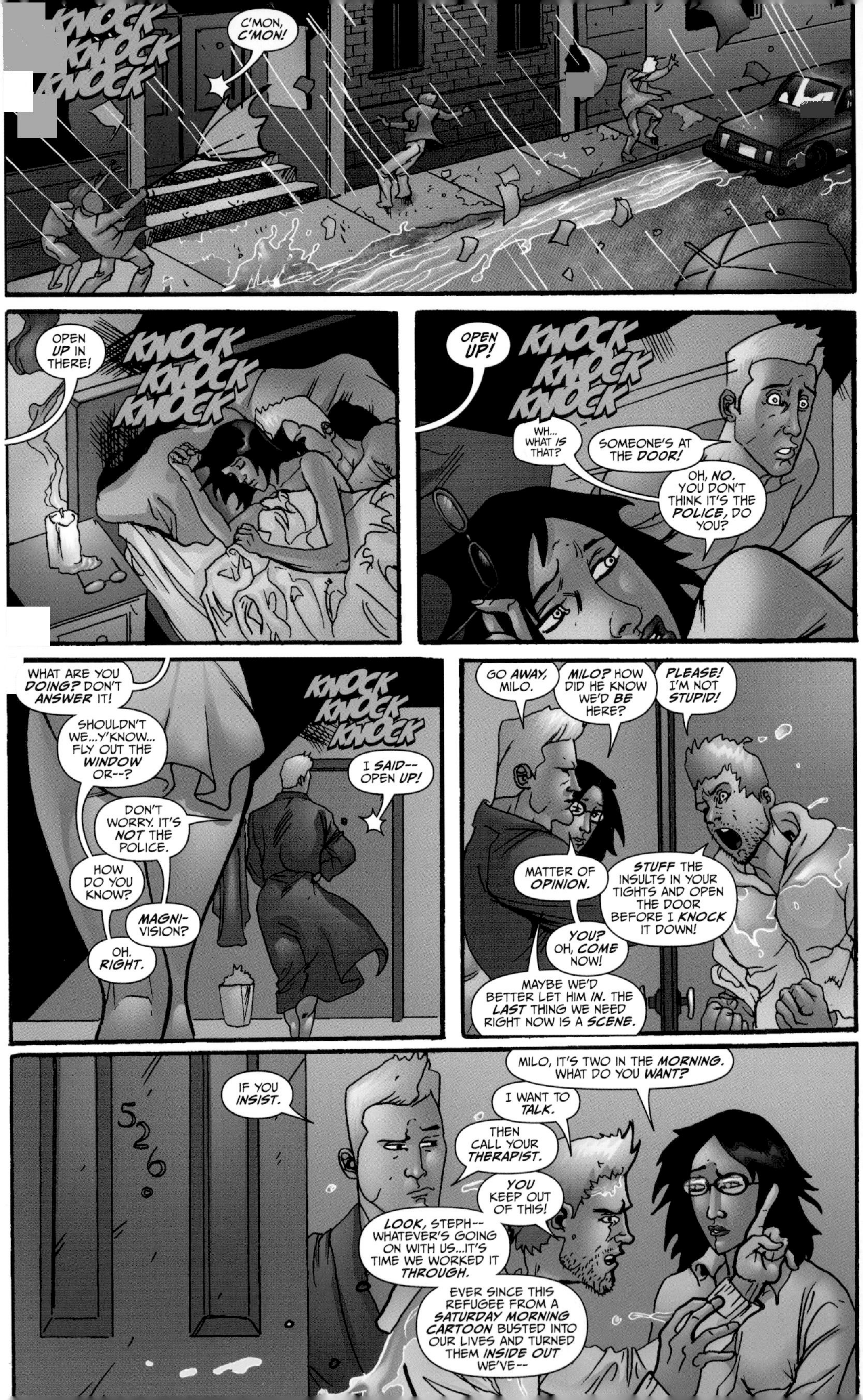
KNOCK KNOCK KNOCK
C'MON, C'MON!
OPEN UP IN THERE!
KNOCK KNOCK KNOCK
OPEN UP!
KNOCK KNOCK KNOCK
WH... WHAT IS THAT?
SOMEONE'S AT THE DOOR!
OH, NO. YOU DON'T THINK IT'S THE POLICE, DO YOU?
WHAT ARE YOU DOING? DON'T ANSWER IT!
SHOULDN'T WE...Y'KNOW... FLY OUT THE WINDOW OR--?
DON'T WORRY. IT'S NOT THE POLICE.
HOW DO YOU KNOW?
MAGNI-VISION?
OH. RIGHT.
KNOCK KNOCK KNOCK
I SAID-- OPEN UP!
GO AWAY, MILO.
MILO? HOW DID HE KNOW WE'D BE HERE?
PLEASE! I'M NOT STUPID!
MATTER OF OPINION.
STUFF THE INSULTS IN YOUR TIGHTS AND OPEN THE DOOR BEFORE I KNOCK IT DOWN!
YOU? OH, COME NOW!
MAYBE WE'D BETTER LET HIM IN. THE LAST THING WE NEED RIGHT NOW IS A SCENE.
IF YOU INSIST.
MILO, IT'S TWO IN THE MORNING. WHAT DO YOU WANT?
I WANT TO TALK.
THEN CALL YOUR THERAPIST.
YOU KEEP OUT OF THIS!
LOOK, STEPH-- WHATEVER'S GOING ON WITH US...IT'S TIME WE WORKED IT THROUGH.
EVER SINCE THIS REFUGEE FROM A SATURDAY MORNING CARTOON BUSTED INTO OUR LIVES AND TURNED THEM INSIDE OUT WE'VE--

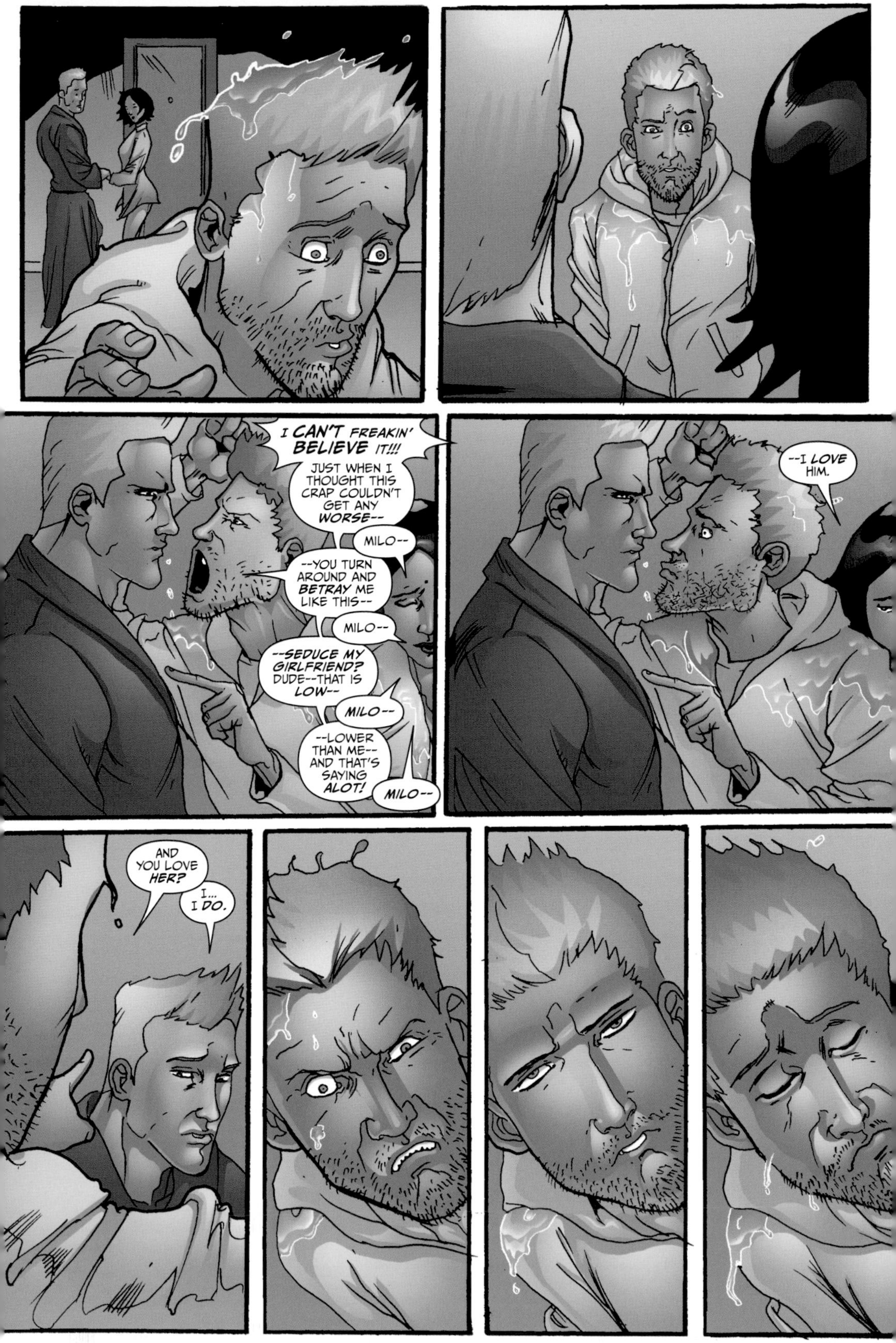
I CAN'T FREAKIN' BELIEVE IT!!! JUST WHEN I THOUGHT THIS CRAP COULDN'T GET ANY WORSE--
MILO--
--YOU TURN AROUND AND BETRAY ME LIKE THIS--
MILO--
--SEDUCE MY GIRLFRIEND? DUDE--THAT IS LOW--
MILO--
--LOWER THAN ME--AND THAT'S SAYING ALOT!
MILO--
--I LOVE HIM.
AND YOU LOVE HER?
I... I DO.

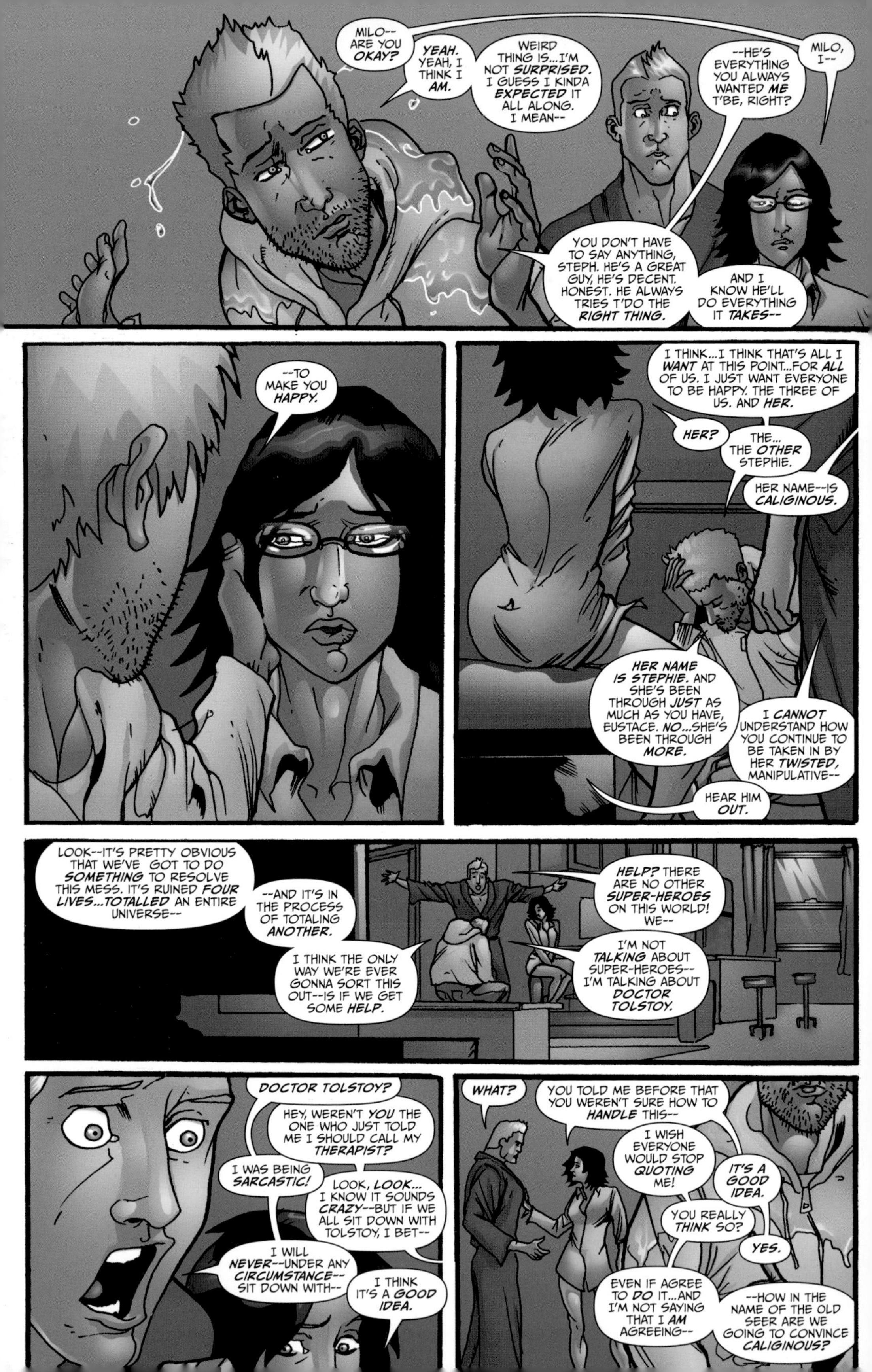
MILO--
ARE YOU OKAY?
YEAH. YEAH, I THINK I AM.
WEIRD THING IS...I'M NOT SURPRISED. I GUESS I KINDA EXPECTED IT ALL ALONG. I MEAN--
--HE'S EVERYTHING YOU ALWAYS WANTED ME T'BE, RIGHT?
MILO, I--
YOU DON'T HAVE TO SAY ANYTHING, STEPH. HE'S A GREAT GUY, HE'S DECENT. HONEST. HE ALWAYS TRIES T'DO THE RIGHT THING.
AND I KNOW HE'LL DO EVERYTHING IT TAKES--
--TO MAKE YOU HAPPY.
I THINK...I THINK THAT'S ALL I WANT AT THIS POINT...FOR ALL OF US. I JUST WANT EVERYONE TO BE HAPPY. THE THREE OF US. AND HER.
HER?
THE... THE OTHER STEPHIE.
HER NAME--IS CALIGINOUS.
HER NAME IS STEPHIE. AND SHE'S BEEN THROUGH JUST AS MUCH AS YOU HAVE, EUSTACE. NO...SHE'S BEEN THROUGH MORE.
I CANNOT UNDERSTAND HOW YOU CONTINUE TO BE TAKEN IN BY HER TWISTED, MANIPULATIVE--
HEAR HIM OUT.
LOOK--IT'S PRETTY OBVIOUS THAT WE'VE GOT TO DO SOMETHING TO RESOLVE THIS MESS. IT'S RUINED FOUR LIVES...TOTALLED AN ENTIRE UNIVERSE--
--AND IT'S IN THE PROCESS OF TOTALING ANOTHER.
I THINK THE ONLY WAY WE'RE EVER GONNA SORT THIS OUT--IS IF WE GET SOME HELP.
HELP? THERE ARE NO OTHER SUPER-HEROES ON THIS WORLD! WE--
I'M NOT TALKING ABOUT SUPER-HEROES-- I'M TALKING ABOUT DOCTOR TOLSTOY.
DOCTOR TOLSTOY?
HEY, WEREN'T YOU THE ONE WHO JUST TOLD ME I SHOULD CALL MY THERAPIST?
I WAS BEING SARCASTIC!
LOOK, LOOK... I KNOW IT SOUNDS CRAZY--BUT IF WE ALL SIT DOWN WITH TOLSTOY, I BET--
I WILL NEVER--UNDER ANY CIRCUMSTANCE-- SIT DOWN WITH--
I THINK IT'S A GOOD IDEA.
WHAT?
YOU TOLD ME BEFORE THAT YOU WEREN'T SURE HOW TO HANDLE THIS--
I WISH EVERYONE WOULD STOP QUOTING ME!
IT'S A GOOD IDEA.
YOU REALLY THINK SO?
YES.
EVEN IF AGREE TO DO IT...AND I'M NOT SAYING THAT I AM AGREEING--
--HOW IN THE NAME OF THE OLD SEER ARE WE GOING TO CONVINCE CALIGINOUS?

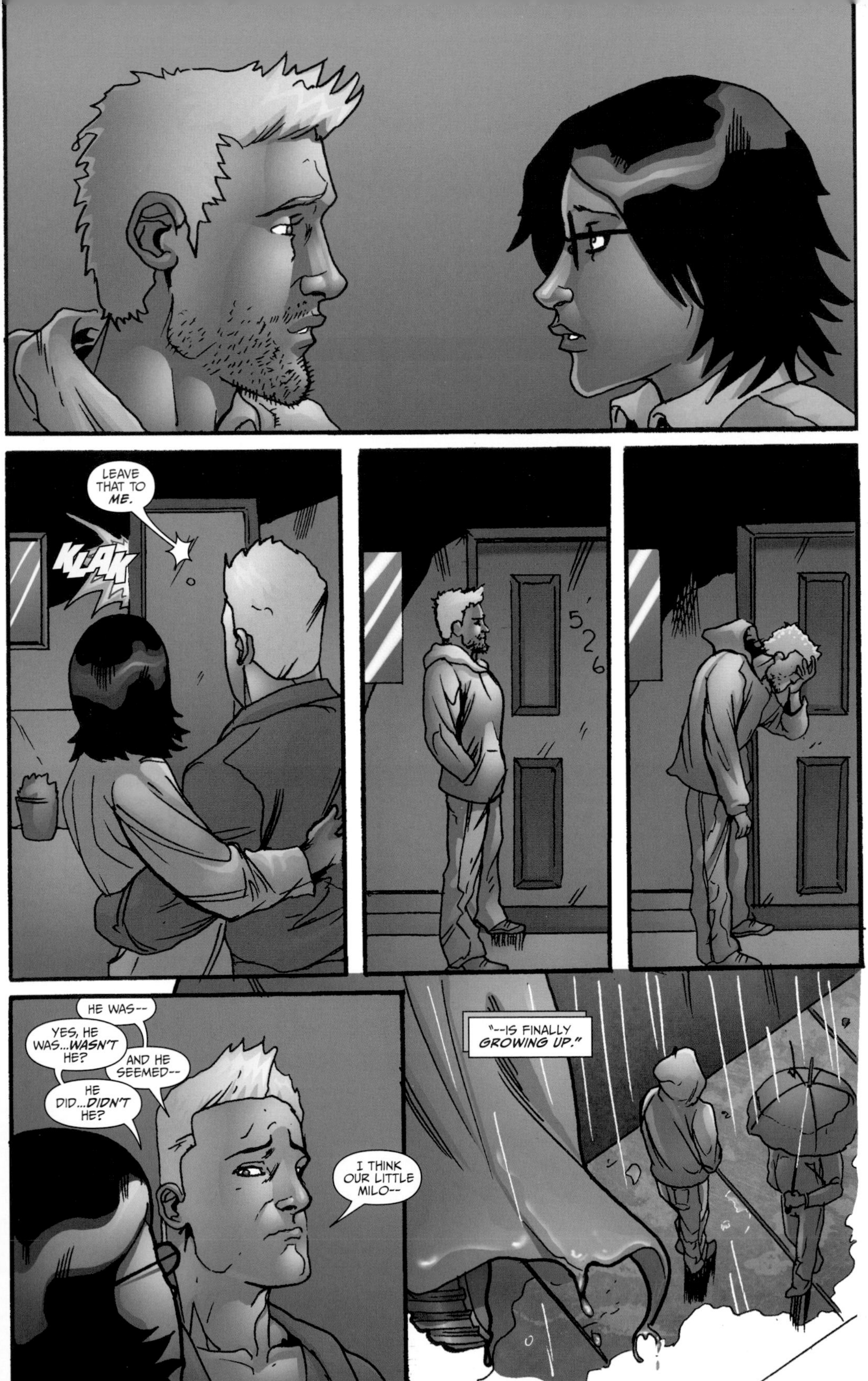
LEAVE THAT TO ME.
KLAK
526
HE WAS--
YES, HE WAS...WASN'T HE?
AND HE SEEMED--
HE DID...DIDN'T HE?
I THINK OUR LITTLE MILO--
"--IS FINALLY GROWING UP."

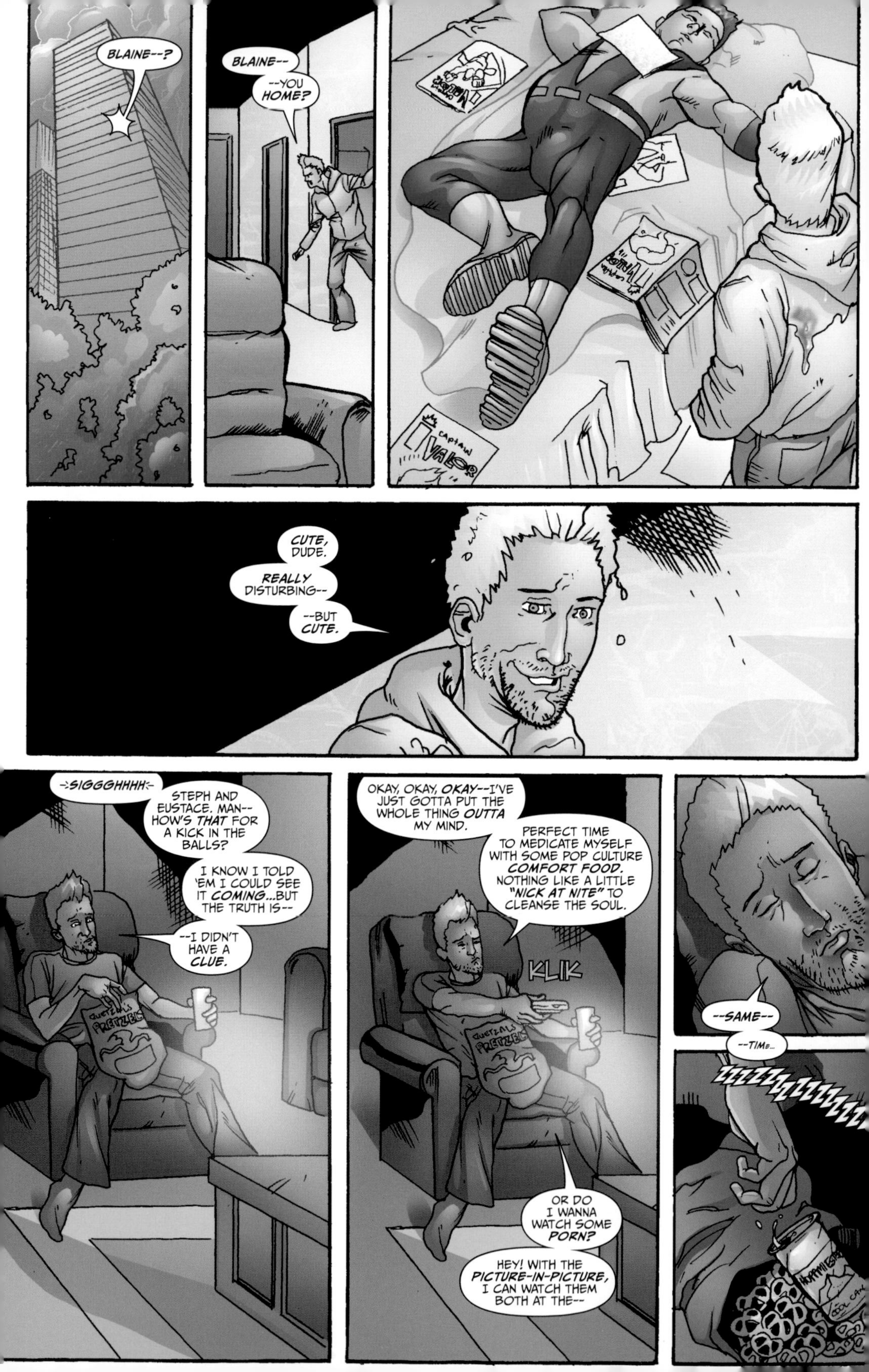
BLAINE--?
BLAINE--
--YOU HOME?
CAPTAIN VALOR
CUTE, DUDE.
REALLY DISTURBING--
--BUT CUTE.
-SIGGGHHHH-
STEPH AND EUSTACE. MAN--HOW'S THAT FOR A KICK IN THE BALLS?
I KNOW I TOLD 'EM I COULD SEE IT COMING...BUT THE TRUTH IS--
--I DIDN'T HAVE A CLUE.
QUETZALS PRETZELS
OKAY, OKAY, OKAY--I'VE JUST GOTTA PUT THE WHOLE THING OUTTA MY MIND.
PERFECT TIME TO MEDICATE MYSELF WITH SOME POP CULTURE COMFORT FOOD. NOTHING LIKE A LITTLE "NICK AT NITE" TO CLEANSE THE SOUL.
KLIK
QUETZALS PRETZELS
OR DO I WANNA WATCH SOME PORN?
HEY! WITH THE PICTURE-IN-PICTURE, I CAN WATCH THEM BOTH AT THE--
--SAME--
--TIME...
ZZZZZZZZZZZZZZZ

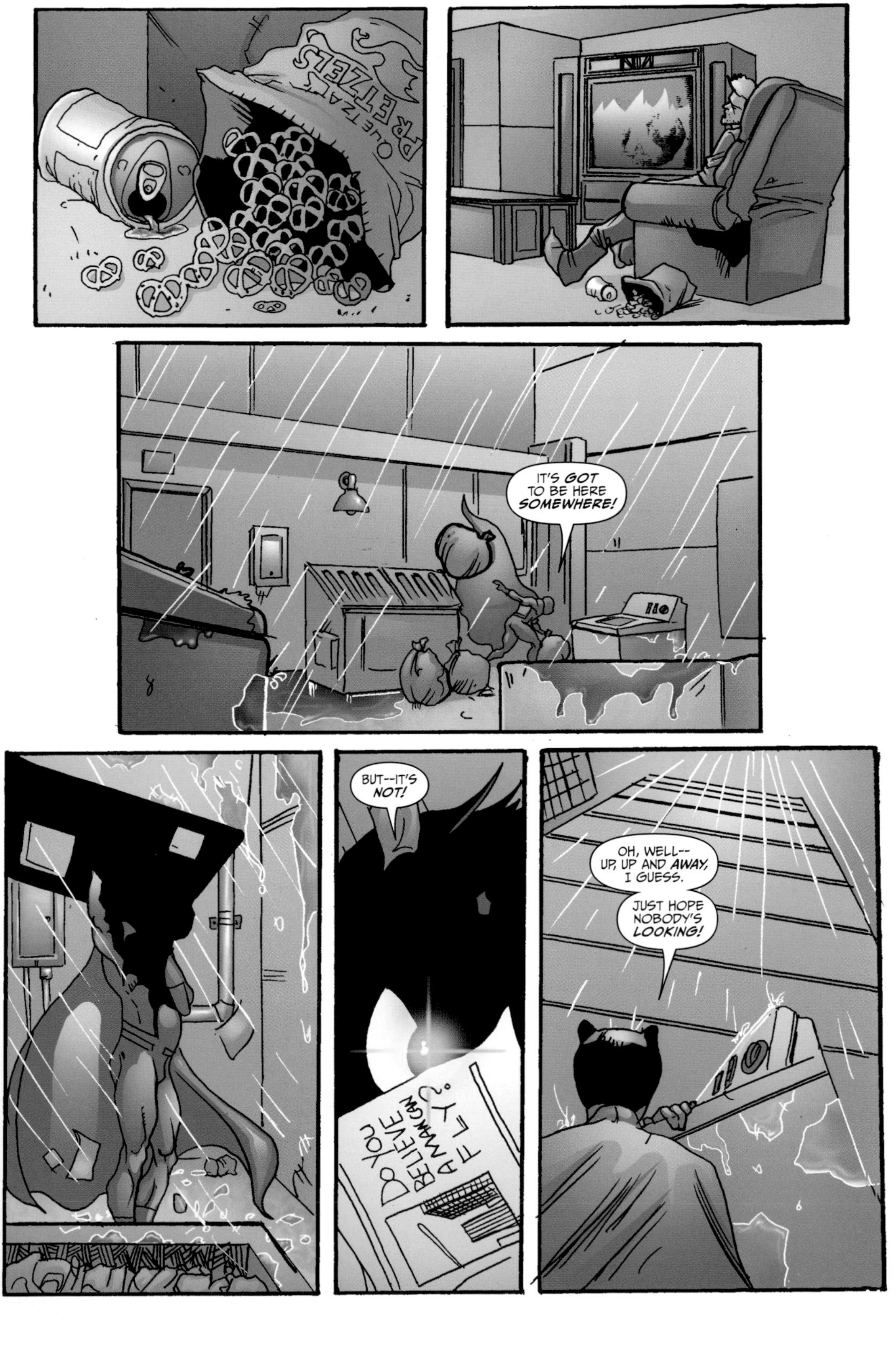
IT'S GOT TO BE HERE SOMEWHERE!
BUT--IT'S NOT!
DO YOU BELIEVE A MAN CAN FLY?
OH, WELL-- UP, UP AND AWAY, I GUESS.
JUST HOPE NOBODY'S LOOKING!

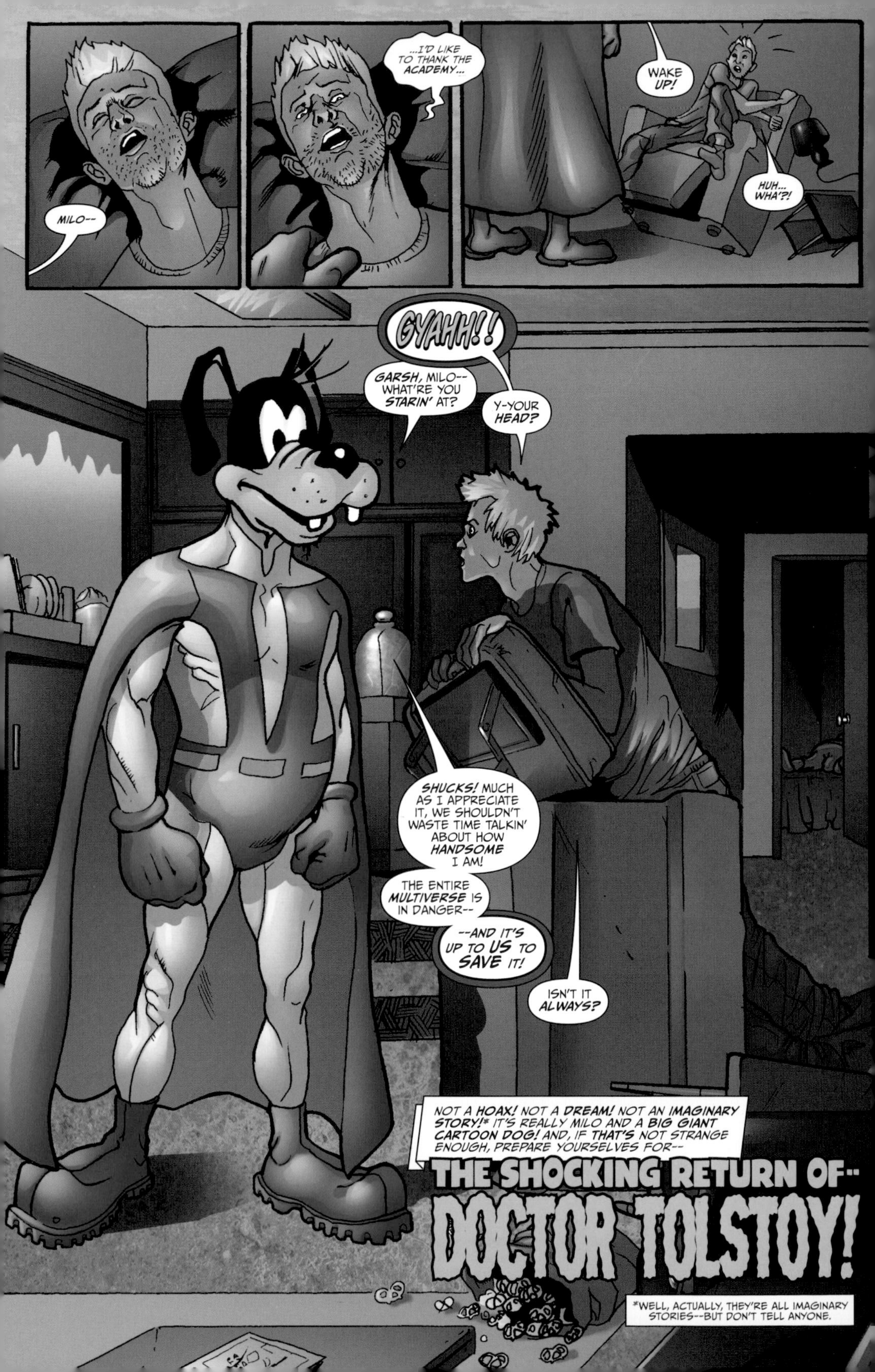
MILO--
...I'D LIKE TO THANK THE ACADEMY...
WAKE UP!
HUH... WHA'?!
GYAHH!!
GARSH, MILO-- WHAT'RE YOU STARIN' AT?
Y-YOUR HEAD?
SHUCKS! MUCH AS I APPRECIATE IT, WE SHOULDN'T WASTE TIME TALKIN' ABOUT HOW HANDSOME I AM!
THE ENTIRE MULTIVERSE IS IN DANGER--
--AND IT'S UP TO US TO SAVE IT!
ISN'T IT ALWAYS?
NOT A HOAX! NOT A DREAM! NOT AN IMAGINARY STORY!* IT'S REALLY MILO AND A BIG GIANT CARTOON DOG! AND, IF THAT'S NOT STRANGE ENOUGH, PREPARE YOURSELVES FOR--
THE SHOCKING RETURN OF--
DOCTOR TOLSTOY!
*WELL, ACTUALLY, THEY'RE ALL IMAGINARY STORIES--BUT DON'T TELL ANYONE.

CHAPTER 2

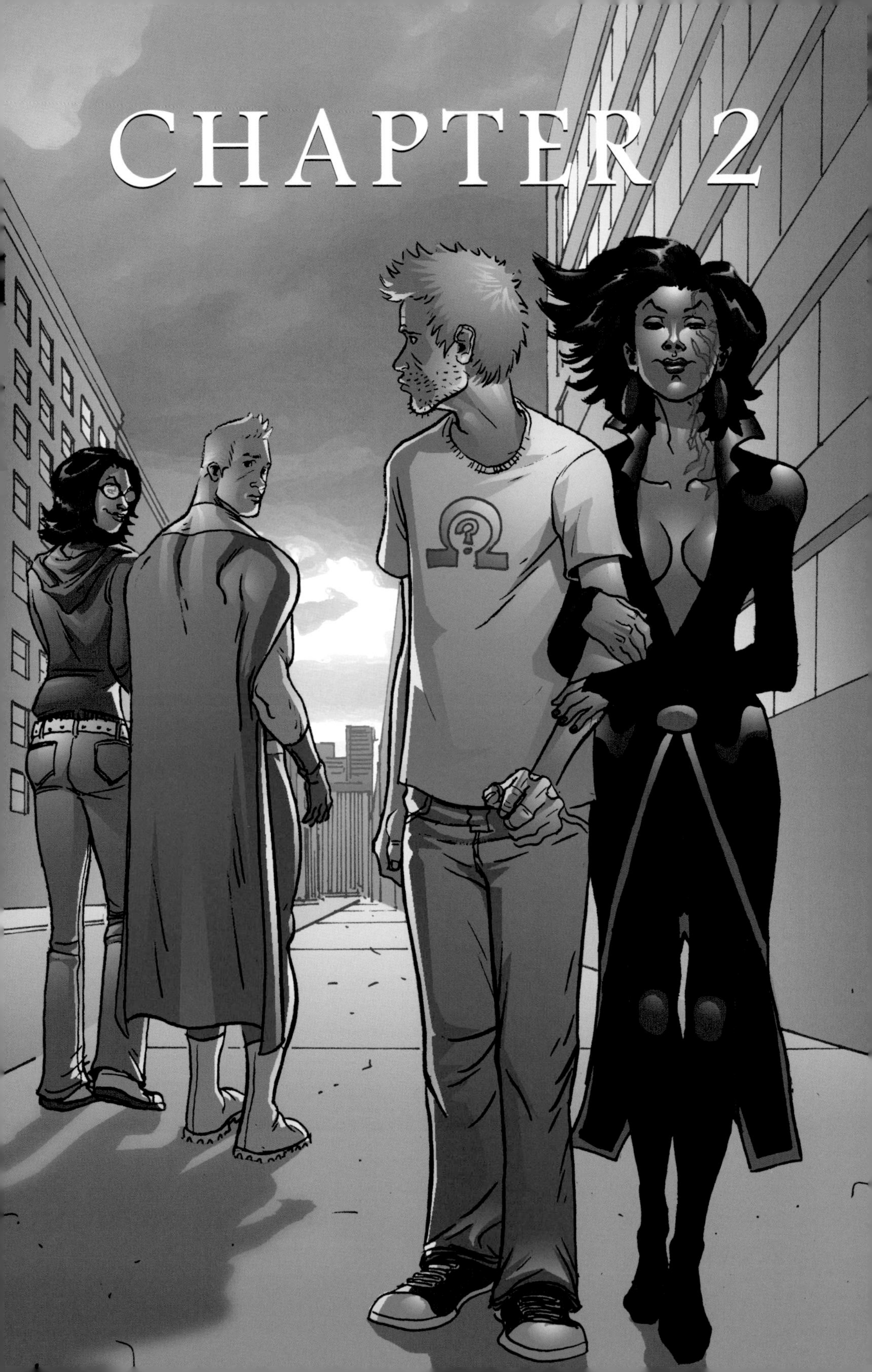

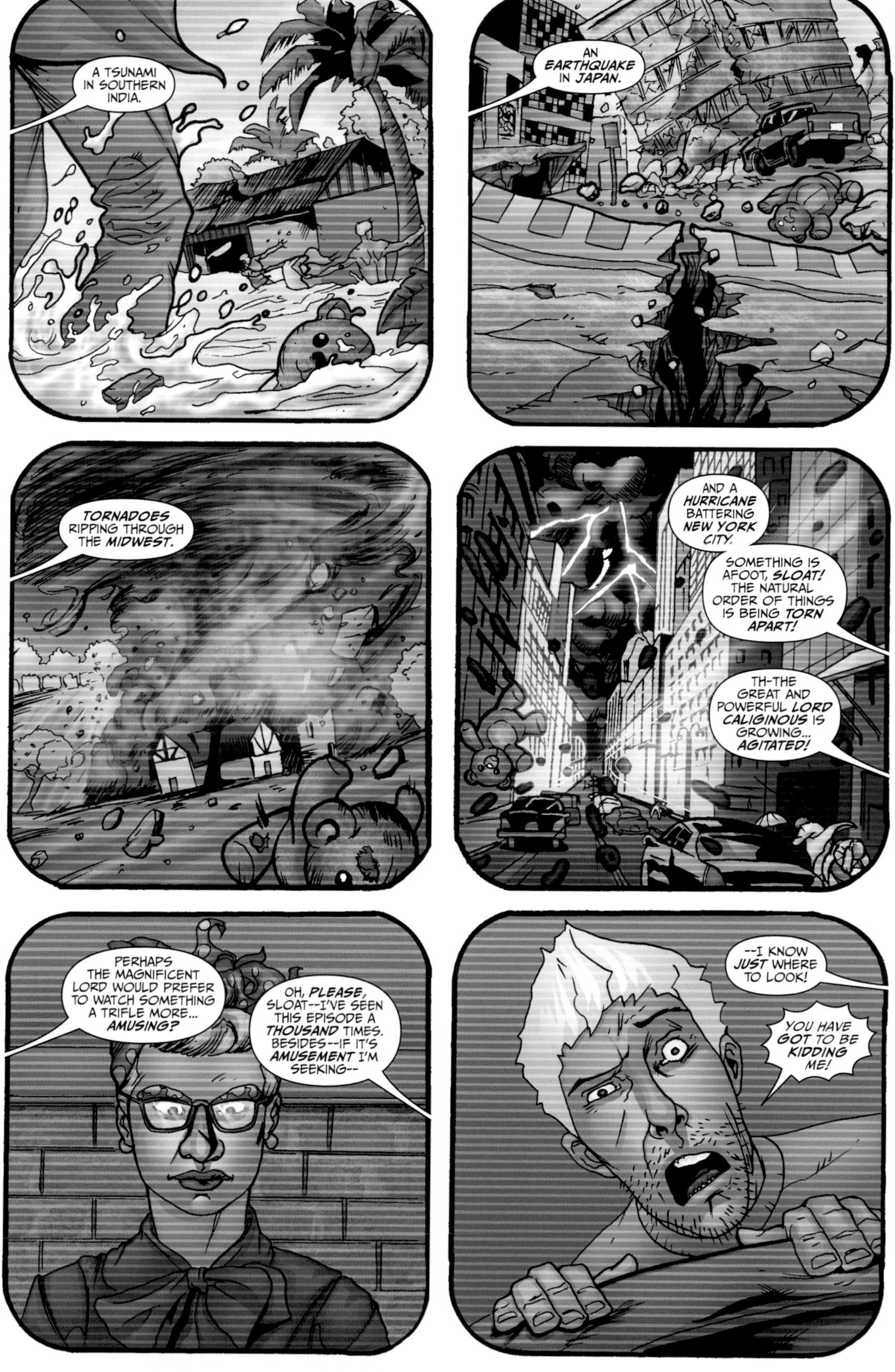
A TSUNAMI IN SOUTHERN INDIA.
AN EARTHQUAKE IN JAPAN.
TORNADOES RIPPING THROUGH THE MIDWEST.
AND A HURRICANE BATTERING NEW YORK CITY.
SOMETHING IS AFOOT, SLOAT! THE NATURAL ORDER OF THINGS IS BEING TORN APART!
TH-THE GREAT AND POWERFUL LORD CALIGINOUS IS GROWING... AGITATED!
PERHAPS THE MAGNIFICENT LORD WOULD PREFER TO WATCH SOMETHING A TRIFLE MORE... AMUSING?
OH, PLEASE, SLOAT--I'VE SEEN THIS EPISODE A THOUSAND TIMES. BESIDES--IF IT'S AMUSEMENT I'M SEEKING--
--I KNOW JUST WHERE TO LOOK!
YOU HAVE GOT TO BE KIDDING ME!

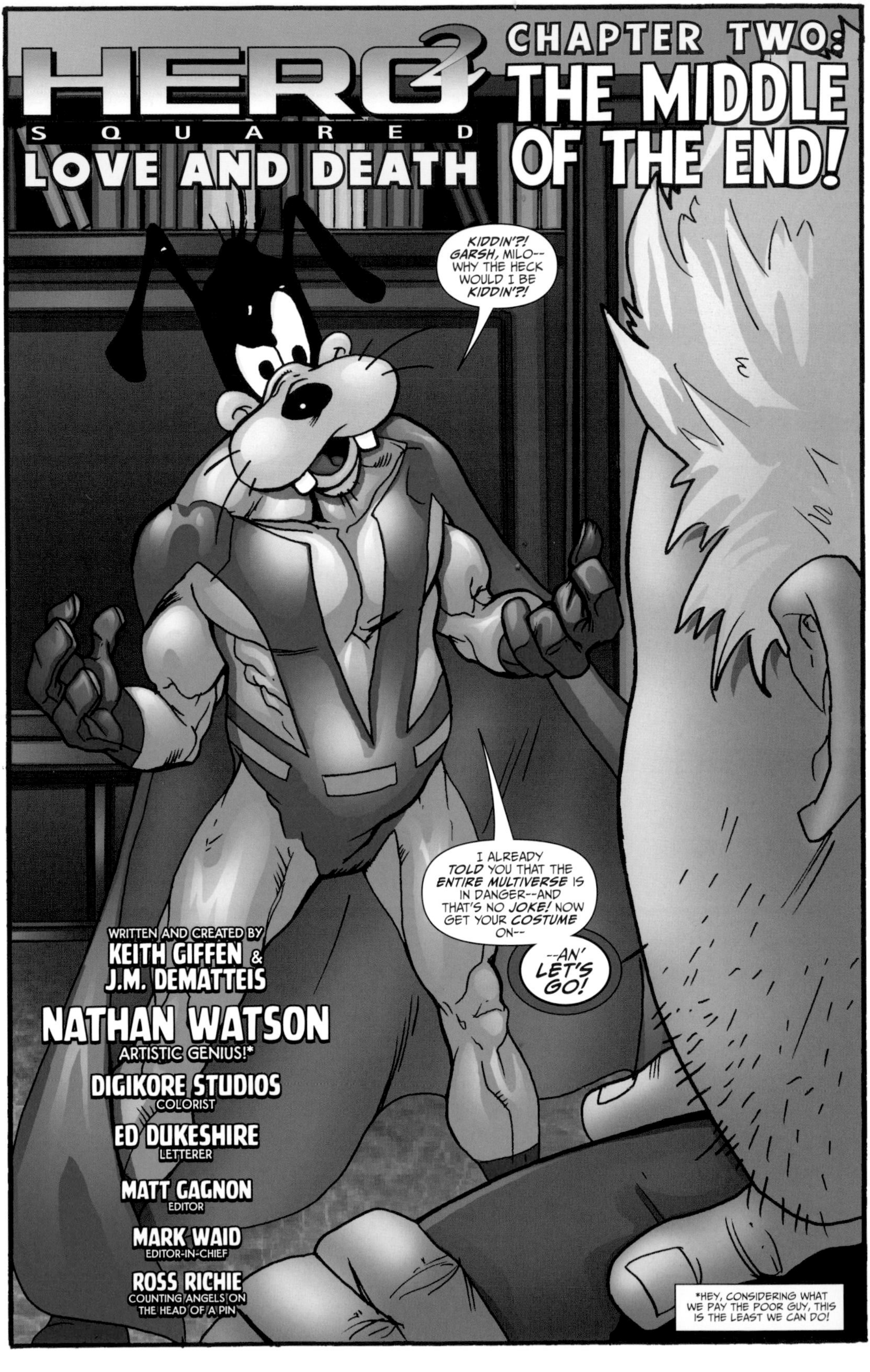
HERO SQUARED
LOVE AND DEATH
CHAPTER TWO:
THE MIDDLE OF THE END!
KIDDIN'?! GARSH, MILO-- WHY THE HECK WOULD I BE KIDDIN'?!
I ALREADY TOLD YOU THAT THE ENTIRE MULTIVERSE IS IN DANGER--AND THAT'S NO JOKE! NOW GET YOUR COSTUME ON--
--AN' LET'S GO!
WRITTEN AND CREATED BY
KEITH GIFFEN & J.M. DEMATTEIS
NATHAN WATSON
ARTISTIC GENIUS!*
DIGIKORE STUDIOS
COLORIST
ED DUKESHIRE
LETTERER
MATT GAGNON
EDITOR
MARK WAID
EDITOR-IN-CHIEF
ROSS RICHIE
COUNTING ANGELS ON THE HEAD OF A PIN
*HEY, CONSIDERING WHAT WE PAY THE POOR GUY, THIS IS THE LEAST WE CAN DO!

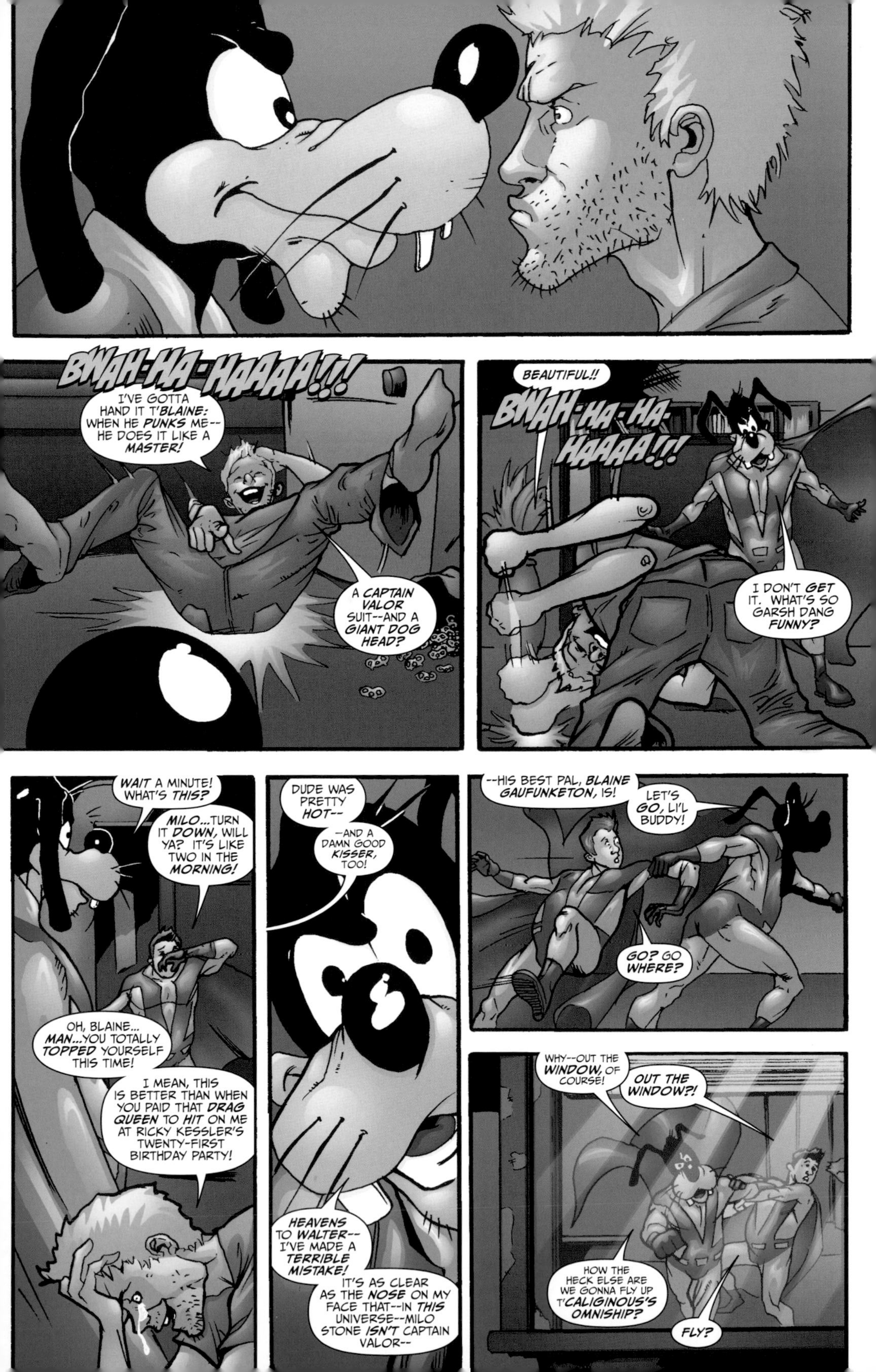
BWAH-HA-HAAAA!!!
I'VE GOTTA HAND IT T'BLAINE: WHEN HE PUNKS ME--HE DOES IT LIKE A MASTER!
A CAPTAIN VALOR SUIT--AND A GIANT DOG HEAD?
BEAUTIFUL!!
BWAH-HA-HA-HAAAA!!!
I DON'T GET IT. WHAT'S SO GARSH DANG FUNNY?
WAIT A MINUTE! WHAT'S THIS?
MILO...TURN IT DOWN, WILL YA? IT'S LIKE TWO IN THE MORNING!
OH, BLAINE... MAN...YOU TOTALLY TOPPED YOURSELF THIS TIME!
I MEAN, THIS IS BETTER THAN WHEN YOU PAID THAT DRAG QUEEN TO HIT ON ME AT RICKY KESSLER'S TWENTY-FIRST BIRTHDAY PARTY!
DUDE WAS PRETTY HOT--
--AND A DAMN GOOD KISSER, TOO!
HEAVENS TO WALTER--I'VE MADE A TERRIBLE MISTAKE!
IT'S AS CLEAR AS THE NOSE ON MY FACE THAT--IN THIS UNIVERSE--MILO STONE ISN'T CAPTAIN VALOR--
--HIS BEST PAL, BLAINE GAUFUNKETON, IS!
LET'S GO, LI'L BUDDY!
GO? GO WHERE?
WHY--OUT THE WINDOW, OF COURSE!
OUT THE WINDOW?!
HOW THE HECK ELSE ARE WE GONNA FLY UP T'CALIGINOUS'S OMNISHIP?
FLY?

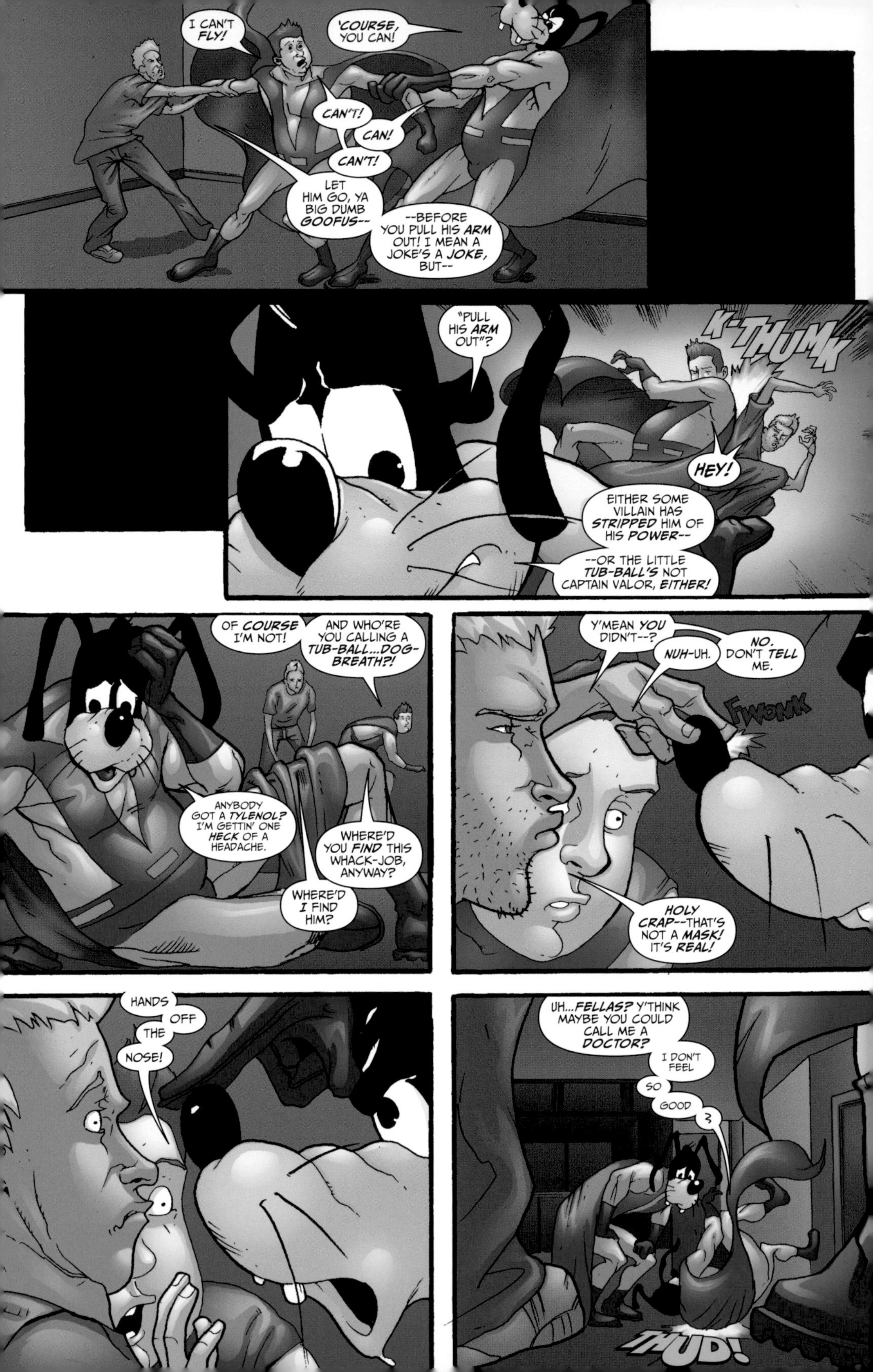
I CAN'T *FLY!*
'*COURSE*, YOU CAN!
CAN'T!
CAN!
CAN'T!
LET HIM GO, YA BIG DUMB *GOOFUS*--
--BEFORE YOU PULL HIS *ARM* OUT! I MEAN A JOKE'S A *JOKE*, BUT--
"PULL HIS *ARM* OUT"?
K-THUMK
HEY!
EITHER SOME VILLAIN HAS *STRIPPED* HIM OF HIS *POWER*--
--OR THE LITTLE *TUB-BALL'S* NOT CAPTAIN VALOR, *EITHER!*
OF *COURSE* I'M NOT!
AND WHO'RE YOU CALLING A *TUB-BALL...DOG-BREATH?!*
ANYBODY GOT A *TYLENOL?* I'M GETTIN' ONE *HECK* OF A HEADACHE.
WHERE'D YOU *FIND* THIS WHACK-JOB, ANYWAY?
WHERE'D *I* FIND HIM?
Y'MEAN *YOU* DIDN'T--?
NUH-UH.
NO. DON'T *TELL* ME.
F'WONK
HOLY CRAP--THAT'S NOT A *MASK!* IT'S *REAL!*
HANDS OFF THE NOSE!
UH...*FELLAS?* Y'THINK MAYBE YOU COULD CALL ME A *DOCTOR?*
I DON'T FEEL SO GOOD
THUD!

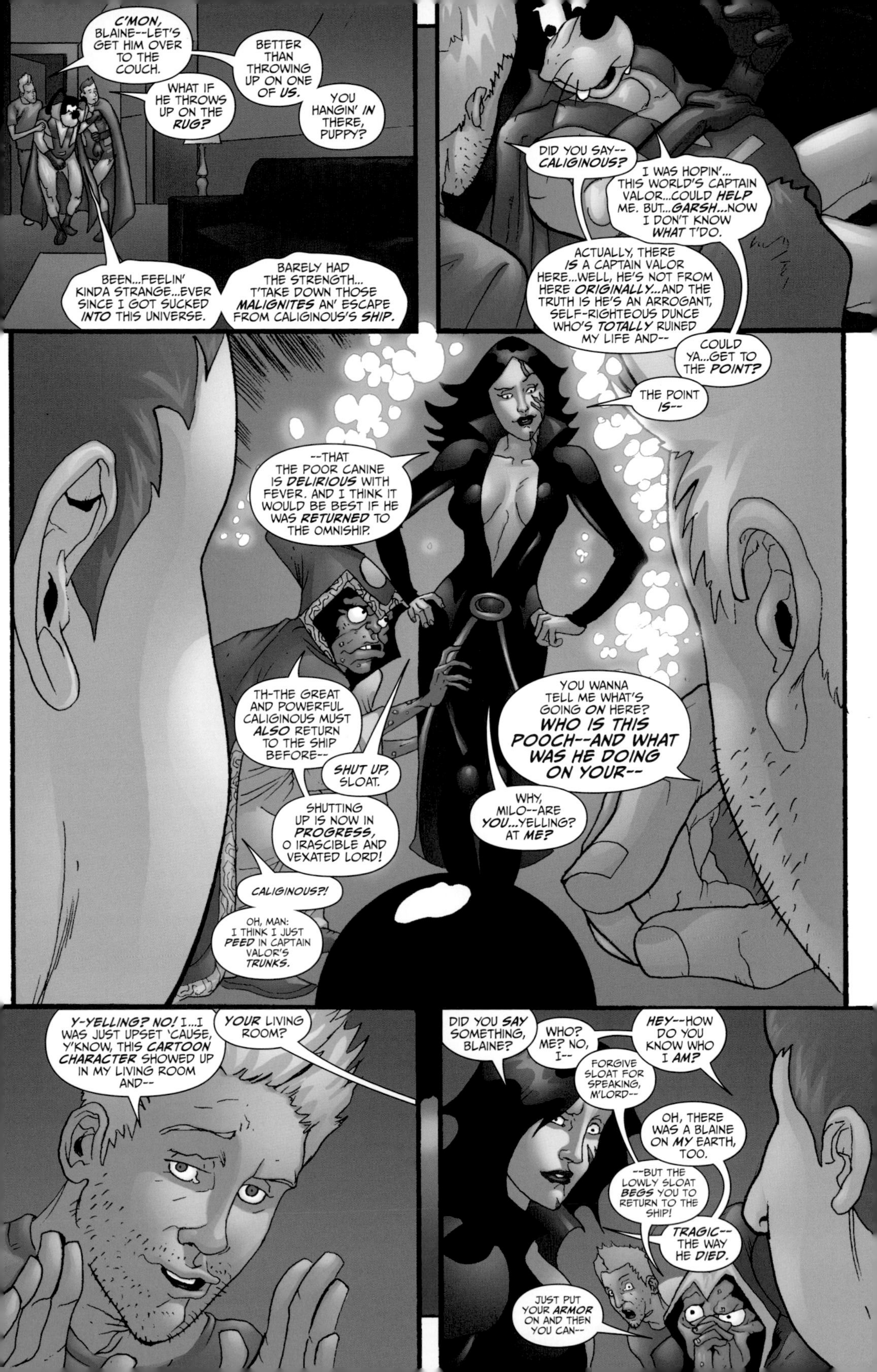
C'MON, BLAINE--LET'S GET HIM OVER TO THE COUCH.
WHAT IF HE THROWS UP ON THE RUG?
BETTER THAN THROWING UP ON ONE OF US.
YOU HANGIN' IN THERE, PUPPY?
BEEN...FEELIN' KINDA STRANGE...EVER SINCE I GOT SUCKED INTO THIS UNIVERSE.
BARELY HAD THE STRENGTH... T'TAKE DOWN THOSE MALIGNITES AN' ESCAPE FROM CALIGINOUS'S SHIP.
DID YOU SAY-- CALIGINOUS?
I WAS HOPIN'... THIS WORLD'S CAPTAIN VALOR...COULD HELP ME. BUT...GARSH...NOW I DON'T KNOW WHAT T'DO.
ACTUALLY, THERE IS A CAPTAIN VALOR HERE...WELL, HE'S NOT FROM HERE ORIGINALLY...AND THE TRUTH IS HE'S AN ARROGANT, SELF-RIGHTEOUS DUNCE WHO'S TOTALLY RUINED MY LIFE AND--
COULD YA...GET TO THE POINT?
THE POINT IS--
--THAT THE POOR CANINE IS DELIRIOUS WITH FEVER. AND I THINK IT WOULD BE BEST IF HE WAS RETURNED TO THE OMNISHIP.
TH-THE GREAT AND POWERFUL CALIGINOUS MUST ALSO RETURN TO THE SHIP BEFORE--
SHUT UP, SLOAT.
SHUTTING UP IS NOW IN PROGRESS, O IRASCIBLE AND VEXATED LORD!
YOU WANNA TELL ME WHAT'S GOING ON HERE? WHO IS THIS POOCH--AND WHAT WAS HE DOING ON YOUR--
WHY, MILO--ARE YOU...YELLING? AT ME?
CALIGINOUS?!
OH, MAN: I JUST THINK I JUST PEED IN CAPTAIN VALOR'S TRUNKS.
Y-YELLING? NO! I...I WAS JUST UPSET 'CAUSE, Y'KNOW, THIS CARTOON CHARACTER SHOWED UP IN MY LIVING ROOM AND--
YOUR LIVING ROOM?
DID YOU SAY SOMETHING, BLAINE?
WHO? ME? NO, I--
HEY--HOW DO YOU KNOW WHO I AM?
FORGIVE SLOAT FOR SPEAKING, M'LORD--
OH, THERE WAS A BLAINE ON MY EARTH, TOO.
--BUT THE LOWLY SLOAT BEGS YOU TO RETURN TO THE SHIP!
TRAGIC-- THE WAY HE DIED.
JUST PUT YOUR ARMOR ON AND THEN YOU CAN--

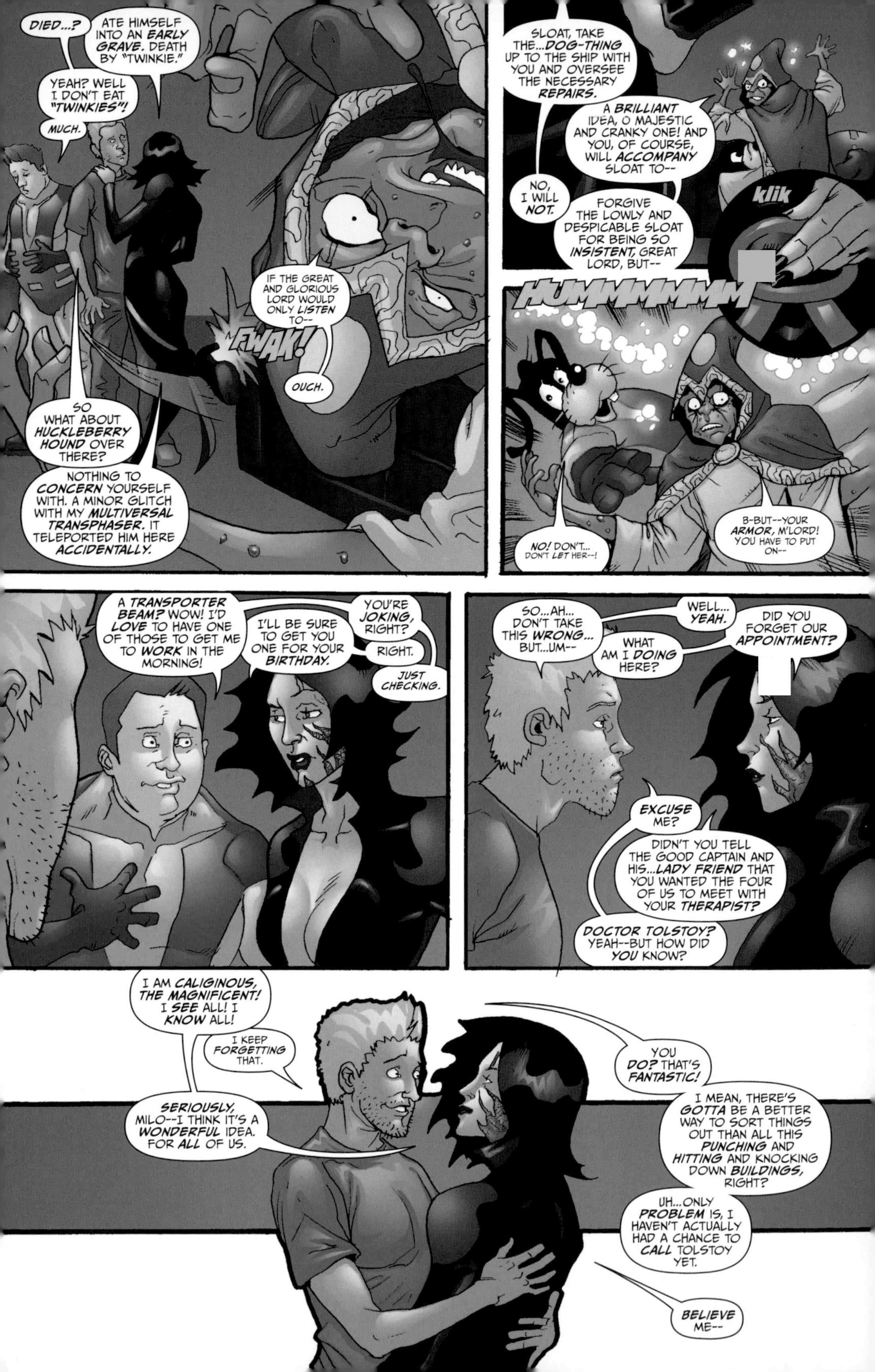

DIED...?
ATE HIMSELF INTO AN EARLY GRAVE. DEATH BY "TWINKIE."
YEAH? WELL I DON'T EAT "TWINKIES"!
MUCH.
IF THE GREAT AND GLORIOUS LORD WOULD ONLY LISTEN TO--
FWAK!
OUCH.
SO WHAT ABOUT HUCKLEBERRY HOUND OVER THERE?
NOTHING TO CONCERN YOURSELF WITH. A MINOR GLITCH WITH MY MULTIVERSAL TRANSPHASER. IT TELEPORTED HIM HERE ACCIDENTALLY.
SLOAT, TAKE THE...DOG-THING UP TO THE SHIP WITH YOU AND OVERSEE THE NECESSARY REPAIRS.
A BRILLIANT IDEA, O MAJESTIC AND CRANKY ONE! AND YOU, OF COURSE, WILL ACCOMPANY SLOAT TO--
NO, I WILL NOT.
FORGIVE THE LOWLY AND DESPICABLE SLOAT FOR BEING SO INSISTENT, GREAT LORD, BUT--
klik
HUMMMMMMM
NO! DON'T... DON'T LET HER--!
B-BUT--YOUR ARMOR, M'LORD! YOU HAVE TO PUT ON--
A TRANSPORTER BEAM? WOW! I'D LOVE TO HAVE ONE OF THOSE TO GET ME TO WORK IN THE MORNING!
I'LL BE SURE TO GET YOU ONE FOR YOUR BIRTHDAY.
YOU'RE JOKING, RIGHT?
RIGHT.
JUST CHECKING.
SO...AH... DON'T TAKE THIS WRONG... BUT...UM--
WELL... YEAH.
WHAT AM I DOING HERE?
DID YOU FORGET OUR APPOINTMENT?
EXCUSE ME?
DIDN'T YOU TELL THE GOOD CAPTAIN AND HIS...LADY FRIEND THAT YOU WANTED THE FOUR OF US TO MEET WITH YOUR THERAPIST?
DOCTOR TOLSTOY? YEAH--BUT HOW DID YOU KNOW?
I AM CALIGINOUS, THE MAGNIFICENT! I SEE ALL! I KNOW ALL!
I KEEP FORGETTING THAT.
SERIOUSLY, MILO--I THINK IT'S A WONDERFUL IDEA. FOR ALL OF US.
YOU DO? THAT'S FANTASTIC!
I MEAN, THERE'S GOTTA BE A BETTER WAY TO SORT THINGS OUT THAN ALL THIS PUNCHING AND HITTING AND KNOCKING DOWN BUILDINGS, RIGHT?
UH...ONLY PROBLEM IS, I HAVEN'T ACTUALLY HAD A CHANCE TO CALL TOLSTOY YET.
BELIEVE ME--

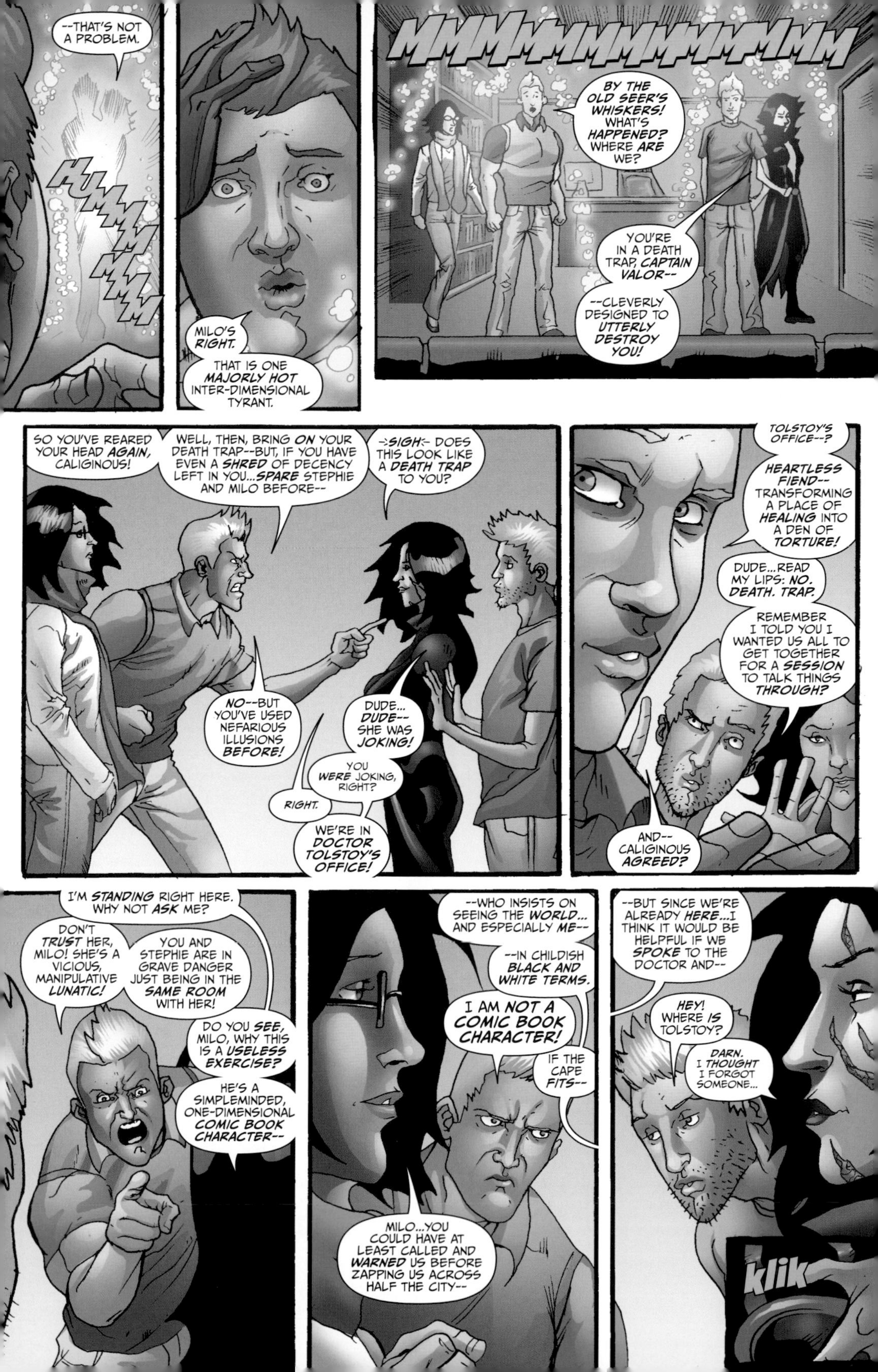
--THAT'S NOT A PROBLEM.
HUMMMMMMM
MILO'S RIGHT.
THAT IS ONE MAJORLY HOT INTER-DIMENSIONAL TYRANT.
MMMMMMMMMMMMMMMM
BY THE OLD SEER'S WHISKERS! WHAT'S HAPPENED? WHERE ARE WE?
YOU'RE IN A DEATH TRAP, CAPTAIN VALOR--
--CLEVERLY DESIGNED TO UTTERLY DESTROY YOU!
SO YOU'VE REARED YOUR HEAD AGAIN, CALIGINOUS!
WELL, THEN, BRING ON YOUR DEATH TRAP--BUT, IF YOU HAVE EVEN A SHRED OF DECENCY LEFT IN YOU...SPARE STEPHIE AND MILO BEFORE--
-SIGH- DOES THIS LOOK LIKE A DEATH TRAP TO YOU?
NO--BUT YOU'VE USED NEFARIOUS ILLUSIONS BEFORE!
DUDE... DUDE-- SHE WAS JOKING!
YOU WERE JOKING, RIGHT?
RIGHT.
WE'RE IN DOCTOR TOLSTOY'S OFFICE!
TOLSTOY'S OFFICE--?
HEARTLESS FIEND-- TRANSFORMING A PLACE OF HEALING INTO A DEN OF TORTURE!
DUDE...READ MY LIPS: NO. DEATH. TRAP.
REMEMBER I TOLD YOU I WANTED US ALL TO GET TOGETHER FOR A SESSION TO TALK THINGS THROUGH?
AND-- CALIGINOUS AGREED?
I'M STANDING RIGHT HERE. WHY NOT ASK ME?
DON'T TRUST HER, MILO! SHE'S A VICIOUS, MANIPULATIVE LUNATIC!
YOU AND STEPHIE ARE IN GRAVE DANGER JUST BEING IN THE SAME ROOM WITH HER!
DO YOU SEE, MILO, WHY THIS IS A USELESS EXERCISE?
HE'S A SIMPLEMINDED, ONE-DIMENSIONAL COMIC BOOK CHARACTER--
--WHO INSISTS ON SEEING THE WORLD... AND ESPECIALLY ME--
--IN CHILDISH BLACK AND WHITE TERMS.
I AM NOT A COMIC BOOK CHARACTER!
IF THE CAPE FITS--
MILO...YOU COULD HAVE AT LEAST CALLED AND WARNED US BEFORE ZAPPING US ACROSS HALF THE CITY--
--BUT SINCE WE'RE ALREADY HERE...I THINK IT WOULD BE HELPFUL IF WE SPOKE TO THE DOCTOR AND--
HEY! WHERE IS TOLSTOY?
DARN. I THOUGHT I FORGOT SOMEONE...
klik

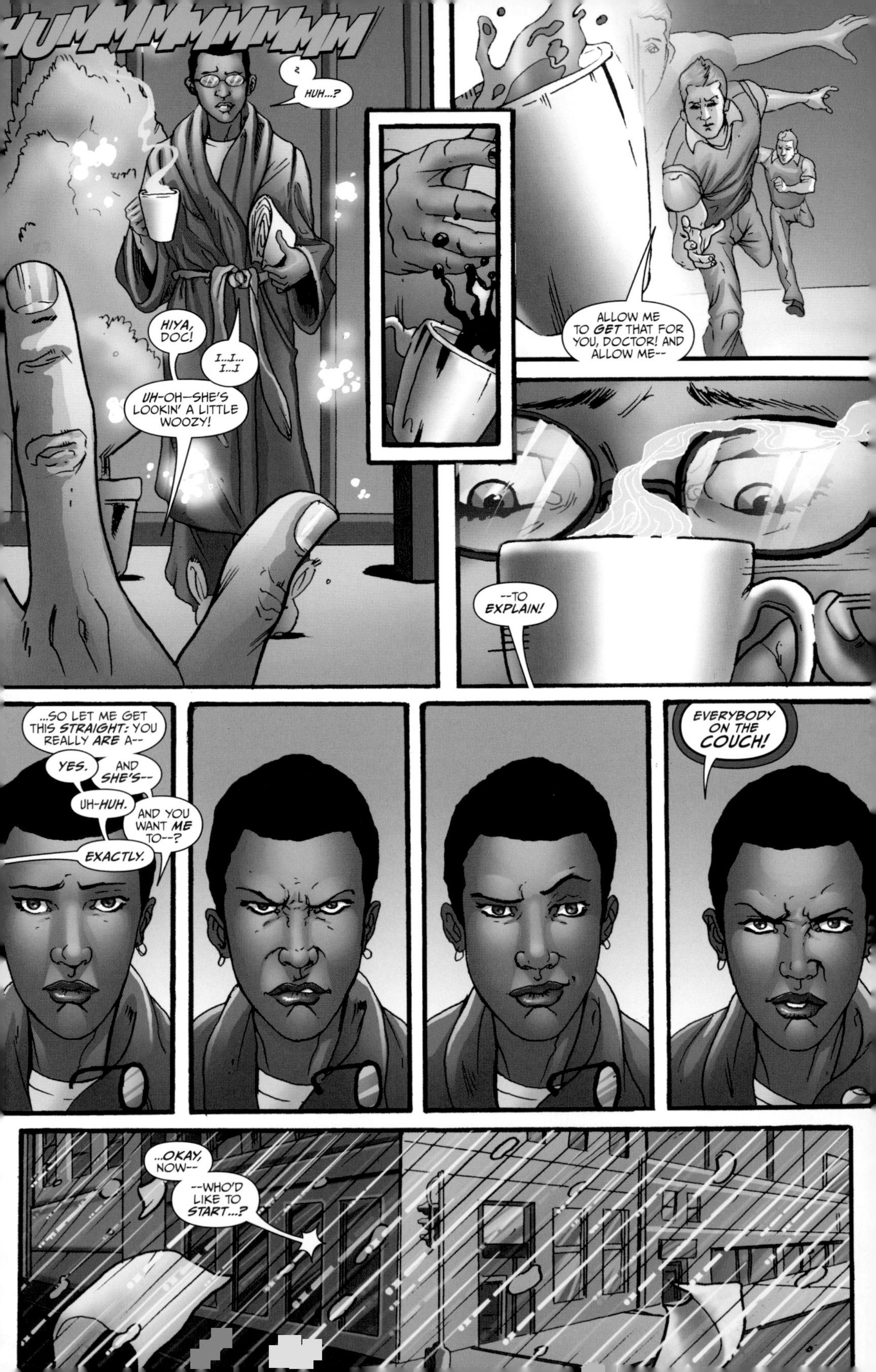
HUMMMMMMMMMM
?
HUH...?
HIYA, DOC!
I...I... I...I
UH-OH--SHE'S LOOKIN' A LITTLE WOOZY!
ALLOW ME TO GET THAT FOR YOU, DOCTOR! AND ALLOW ME--
--TO EXPLAIN!
...SO LET ME GET THIS STRAIGHT: YOU REALLY ARE A--
YES.
AND SHE'S--
UH-HUH.
AND YOU WANT ME TO--?
EXACTLY.
EVERYBODY ON THE COUCH!
...OKAY, NOW--
--WHO'D LIKE TO START...?

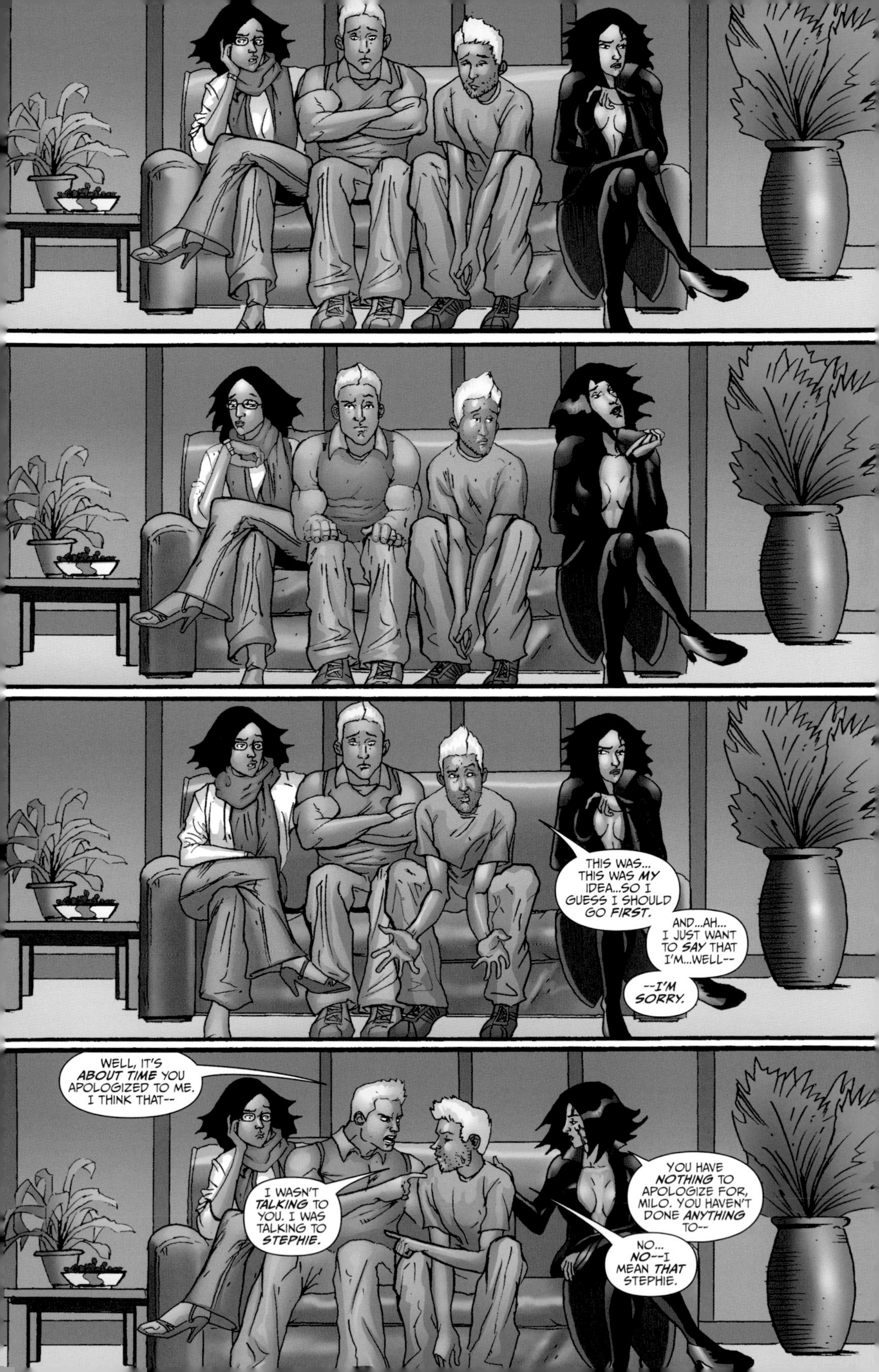
THIS WAS... THIS WAS *MY* IDEA...SO I GUESS I SHOULD GO *FIRST.*
AND...AH... I JUST WANT TO *SAY* THAT I'M...WELL--
--I'M SORRY.
WELL, IT'S *ABOUT TIME* YOU APOLOGIZED TO ME. I THINK THAT--
I WASN'T *TALKING* TO YOU. I WAS TALKING TO *STEPHIE.*
YOU HAVE *NOTHING* TO APOLOGIZE FOR, MILO. YOU HAVEN'T DONE *ANYTHING* TO--
NO... *NO*--I MEAN *THAT* STEPHIE.

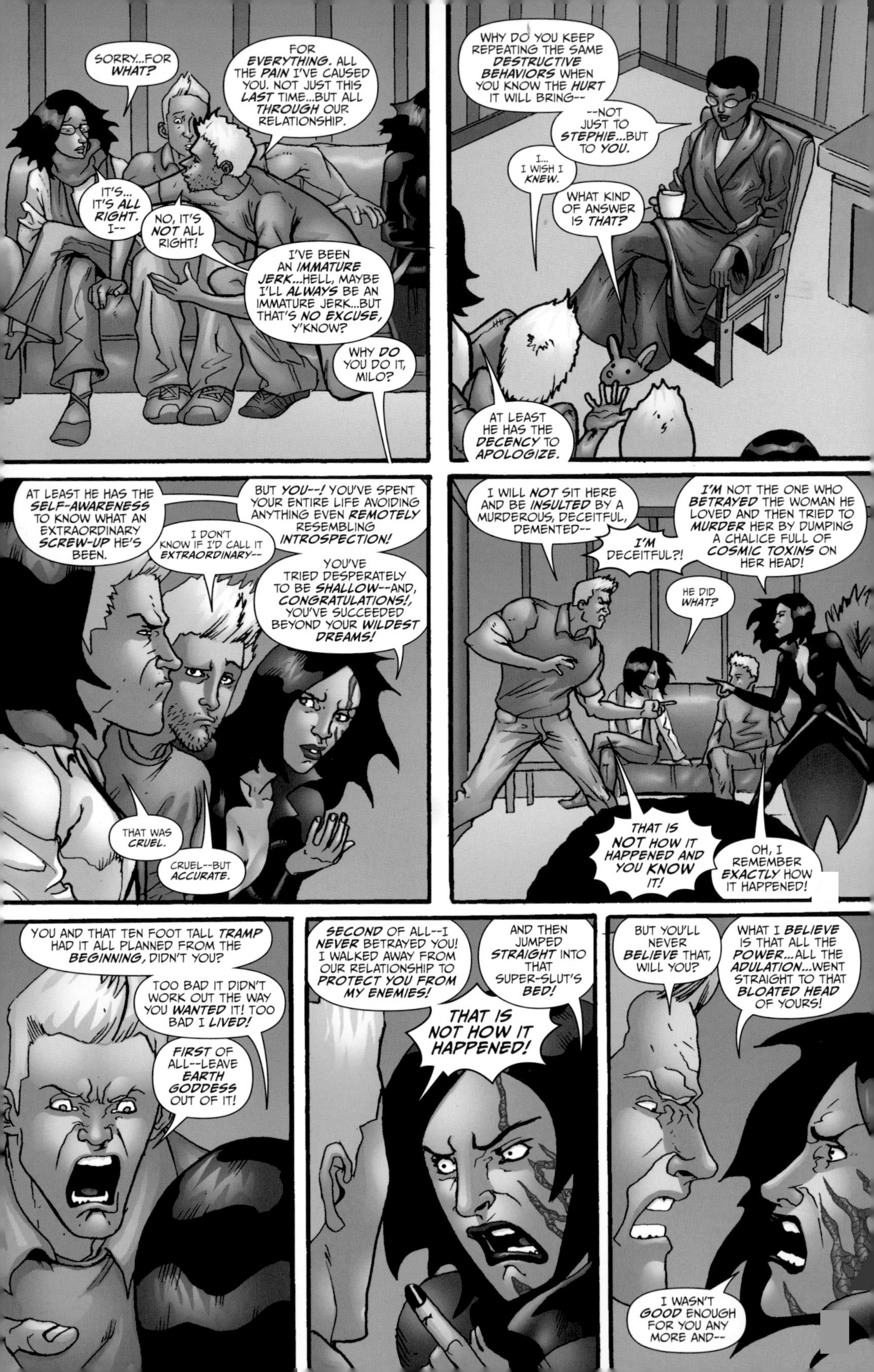
SORRY...FOR WHAT?
FOR EVERYTHING. ALL THE PAIN I'VE CAUSED YOU. NOT JUST THIS LAST TIME...BUT ALL THROUGH OUR RELATIONSHIP.
IT'S... IT'S ALL RIGHT. I--
NO, IT'S NOT ALL RIGHT!
I'VE BEEN AN IMMATURE JERK...HELL, MAYBE I'LL ALWAYS BE AN IMMATURE JERK...BUT THAT'S NO EXCUSE, Y'KNOW?
WHY DO YOU DO IT, MILO?
WHY DO YOU KEEP REPEATING THE SAME DESTRUCTIVE BEHAVIORS WHEN YOU KNOW THE HURT IT WILL BRING--
--NOT JUST TO STEPHIE...BUT TO YOU.
I... I WISH I KNEW.
WHAT KIND OF ANSWER IS THAT?
AT LEAST HE HAS THE DECENCY TO APOLOGIZE.
AT LEAST HE HAS THE SELF-AWARENESS TO KNOW WHAT AN EXTRAORDINARY SCREW-UP HE'S BEEN.
I DON'T KNOW IF I'D CALL IT EXTRAORDINARY--
BUT YOU--! YOU'VE SPENT YOUR ENTIRE LIFE AVOIDING ANYTHING EVEN REMOTELY RESEMBLING INTROSPECTION!
YOU'VE TRIED DESPERATELY TO BE SHALLOW--AND, CONGRATULATIONS!, YOU'VE SUCCEEDED BEYOND YOUR WILDEST DREAMS!
THAT WAS CRUEL.
CRUEL--BUT ACCURATE.
I WILL NOT SIT HERE AND BE INSULTED BY A MURDEROUS, DECEITFUL, DEMENTED--
I'M DECEITFUL?!
I'M NOT THE ONE WHO BETRAYED THE WOMAN HE LOVED AND THEN TRIED TO MURDER HER BY DUMPING A CHALICE FULL OF COSMIC TOXINS ON HER HEAD!
HE DID WHAT?
THAT IS NOT HOW IT HAPPENED AND YOU KNOW IT!
OH, I REMEMBER EXACTLY HOW IT HAPPENED!
YOU AND THAT TEN FOOT TALL TRAMP HAD IT ALL PLANNED FROM THE BEGINNING, DIDN'T YOU?
TOO BAD IT DIDN'T WORK OUT THE WAY YOU WANTED IT! TOO BAD I LIVED!
FIRST OF ALL--LEAVE EARTH GODDESS OUT OF IT!
SECOND OF ALL--I NEVER BETRAYED YOU! I WALKED AWAY FROM OUR RELATIONSHIP TO PROTECT YOU FROM MY ENEMIES!
AND THEN JUMPED STRAIGHT INTO THAT SUPER-SLUT'S BED!
THAT IS NOT HOW IT HAPPENED!
BUT YOU'LL NEVER BELIEVE THAT, WILL YOU?
WHAT I BELIEVE IS THAT ALL THE POWER...ALL THE ADULATION...WENT STRAIGHT TO THAT BLOATED HEAD OF YOURS!
I WASN'T GOOD ENOUGH FOR YOU ANY MORE AND--

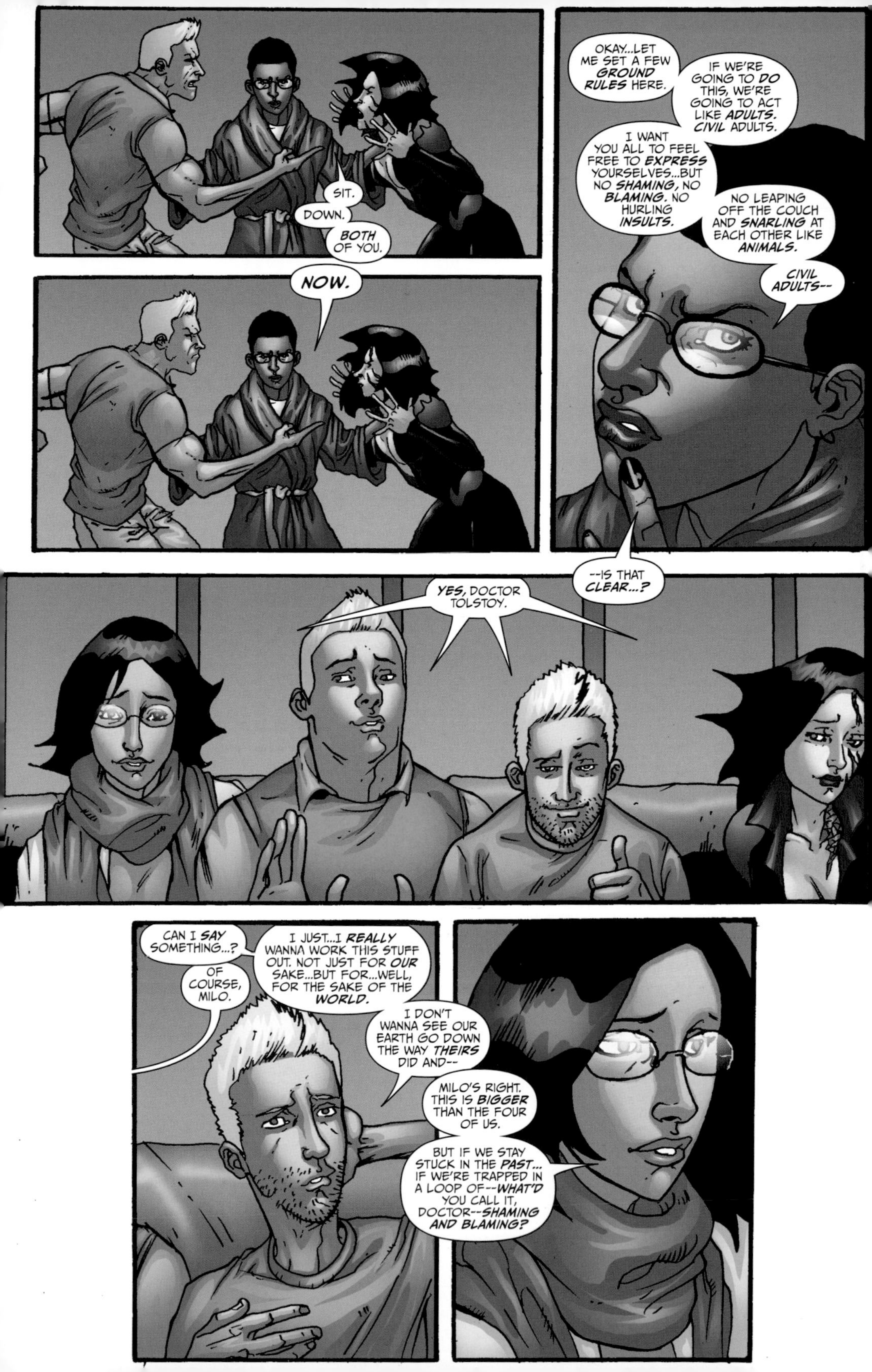

SIT.
DOWN.
BOTH OF YOU.
NOW.
OKAY...LET ME SET A FEW GROUND RULES HERE.
IF WE'RE GOING TO DO THIS, WE'RE GOING TO ACT LIKE ADULTS. CIVIL ADULTS.
I WANT YOU ALL TO FEEL FREE TO EXPRESS YOURSELVES...BUT NO SHAMING, NO BLAMING. NO HURLING INSULTS.
NO LEAPING OFF THE COUCH AND SNARLING AT EACH OTHER LIKE ANIMALS.
CIVIL ADULTS--
--IS THAT CLEAR...?
YES, DOCTOR TOLSTOY.
CAN I SAY SOMETHING...?
OF COURSE, MILO.
I JUST...I REALLY WANNA WORK THIS STUFF OUT. NOT JUST FOR OUR SAKE...BUT FOR...WELL, FOR THE SAKE OF THE WORLD.
I DON'T WANNA SEE OUR EARTH GO DOWN THE WAY THEIRS DID AND--
MILO'S RIGHT. THIS IS BIGGER THAN THE FOUR OF US.
BUT IF WE STAY STUCK IN THE PAST... IF WE'RE TRAPPED IN A LOOP OF--WHAT'D YOU CALL IT, DOCTOR--SHAMING AND BLAMING?

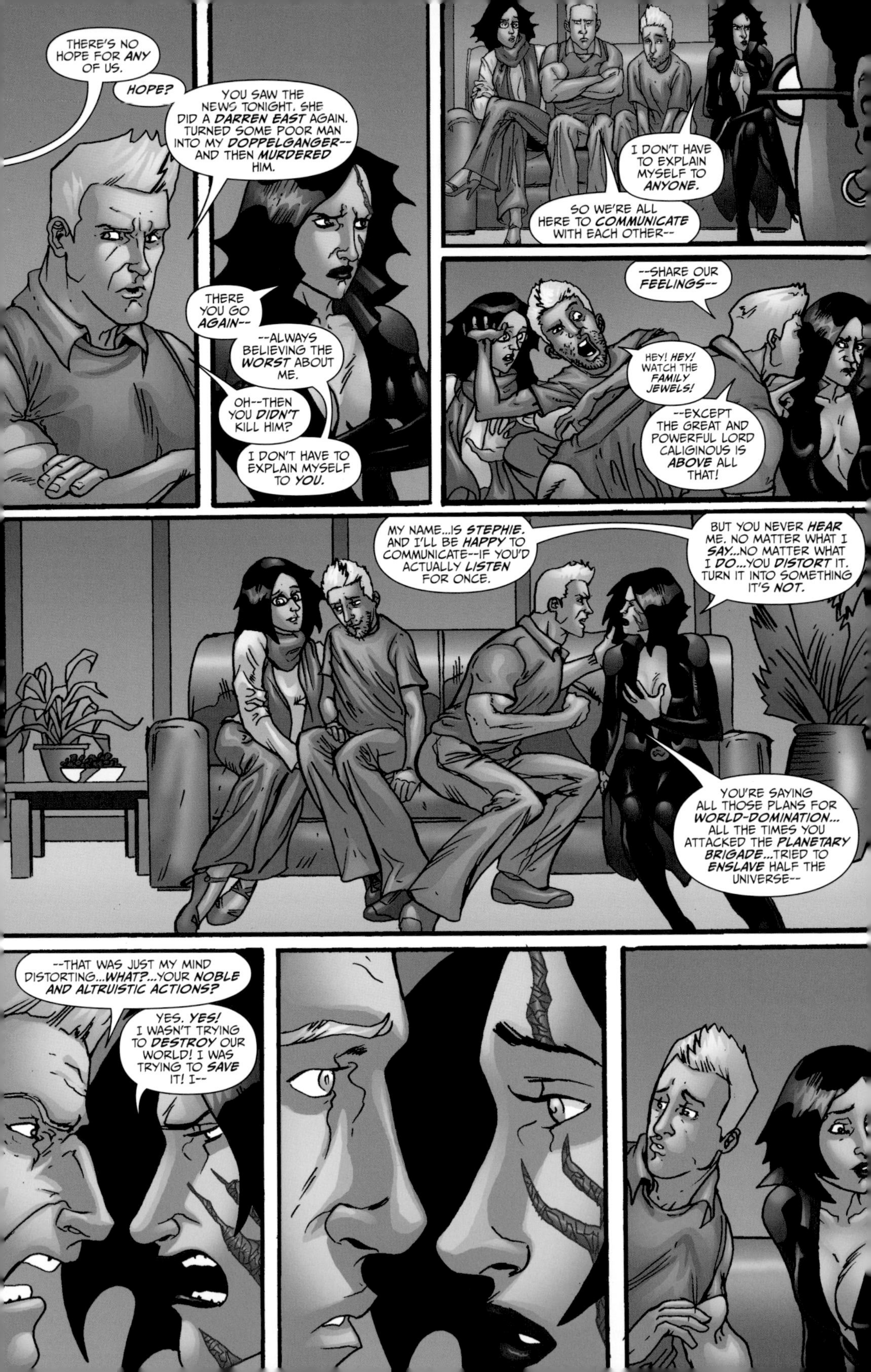
THERE'S NO HOPE FOR ANY OF US.
HOPE?
YOU SAW THE NEWS TONIGHT. SHE DID A DARREN EAST AGAIN. TURNED SOME POOR MAN INTO MY DOPPELGANGER-- AND THEN MURDERED HIM.
THERE YOU GO AGAIN--
--ALWAYS BELIEVING THE WORST ABOUT ME.
OH--THEN YOU DIDN'T KILL HIM?
I DON'T HAVE TO EXPLAIN MYSELF TO YOU.
I DON'T HAVE TO EXPLAIN MYSELF TO ANYONE.
SO WE'RE ALL HERE TO COMMUNICATE WITH EACH OTHER--
--SHARE OUR FEELINGS--
HEY! HEY! WATCH THE FAMILY JEWELS!
--EXCEPT THE GREAT AND POWERFUL LORD CALIGINOUS IS ABOVE ALL THAT!
MY NAME...IS STEPHIE. AND I'LL BE HAPPY TO COMMUNICATE--IF YOU'D ACTUALLY LISTEN FOR ONCE.
BUT YOU NEVER HEAR ME. NO MATTER WHAT I SAY...NO MATTER WHAT I DO...YOU DISTORT IT. TURN IT INTO SOMETHING IT'S NOT.
YOU'RE SAYING ALL THOSE PLANS FOR WORLD-DOMINATION... ALL THE TIMES YOU ATTACKED THE PLANETARY BRIGADE...TRIED TO ENSLAVE HALF THE UNIVERSE--
--THAT WAS JUST MY MIND DISTORTING...WHAT?...YOUR NOBLE AND ALTRUISTIC ACTIONS?
YES. YES! I WASN'T TRYING TO DESTROY OUR WORLD! I WAS TRYING TO SAVE IT! I--

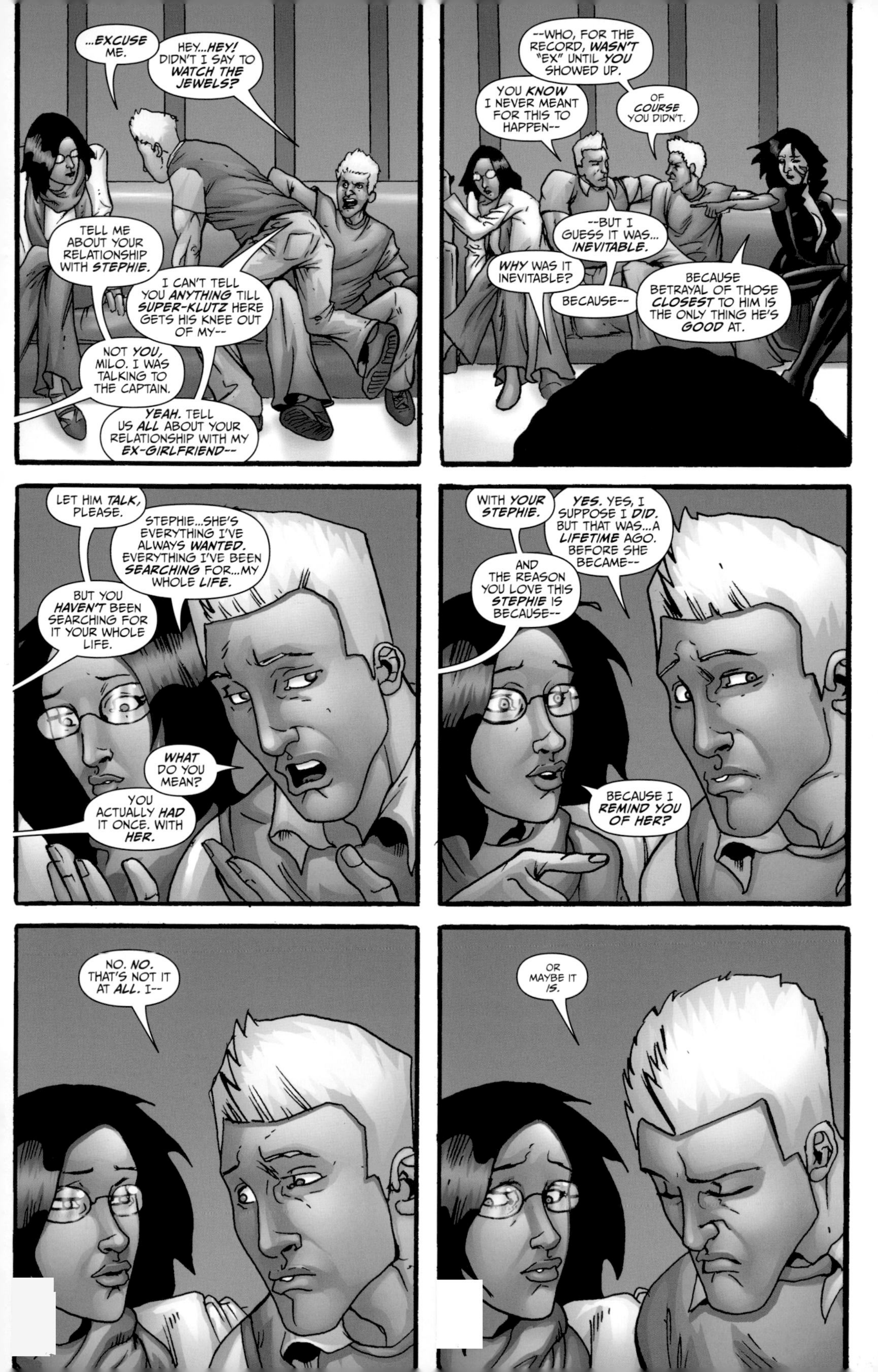

...EXCUSE ME.
HEY...HEY! DIDN'T I SAY TO WATCH THE JEWELS?
TELL ME ABOUT YOUR RELATIONSHIP WITH STEPHIE.
I CAN'T TELL YOU ANYTHING TILL SUPER-KLUTZ HERE GETS HIS KNEE OUT OF MY--
NOT YOU, MILO. I WAS TALKING TO THE CAPTAIN.
YEAH. TELL US ALL ABOUT YOUR RELATIONSHIP WITH MY EX-GIRLFRIEND--
--WHO, FOR THE RECORD, WASN'T "EX" UNTIL YOU SHOWED UP.
YOU KNOW I NEVER MEANT FOR THIS TO HAPPEN--
OF COURSE YOU DIDN'T.
--BUT I GUESS IT WAS... INEVITABLE.
WHY WAS IT INEVITABLE?
BECAUSE--
BECAUSE BETRAYAL OF THOSE CLOSEST TO HIM IS THE ONLY THING HE'S GOOD AT.
LET HIM TALK, PLEASE.
STEPHIE...SHE'S EVERYTHING I'VE ALWAYS WANTED. EVERYTHING I'VE BEEN SEARCHING FOR...MY WHOLE LIFE.
BUT YOU HAVEN'T BEEN SEARCHING FOR IT YOUR WHOLE LIFE.
WHAT DO YOU MEAN?
YOU ACTUALLY HAD IT ONCE. WITH HER.
WITH YOUR STEPHIE.
YES. YES, I SUPPOSE I DID. BUT THAT WAS...A LIFETIME AGO. BEFORE SHE BECAME--
AND THE REASON YOU LOVE THIS STEPHIE IS BECAUSE--
BECAUSE I REMIND YOU OF HER?
NO. NO. THAT'S NOT IT AT ALL. I--
OR MAYBE IT IS.

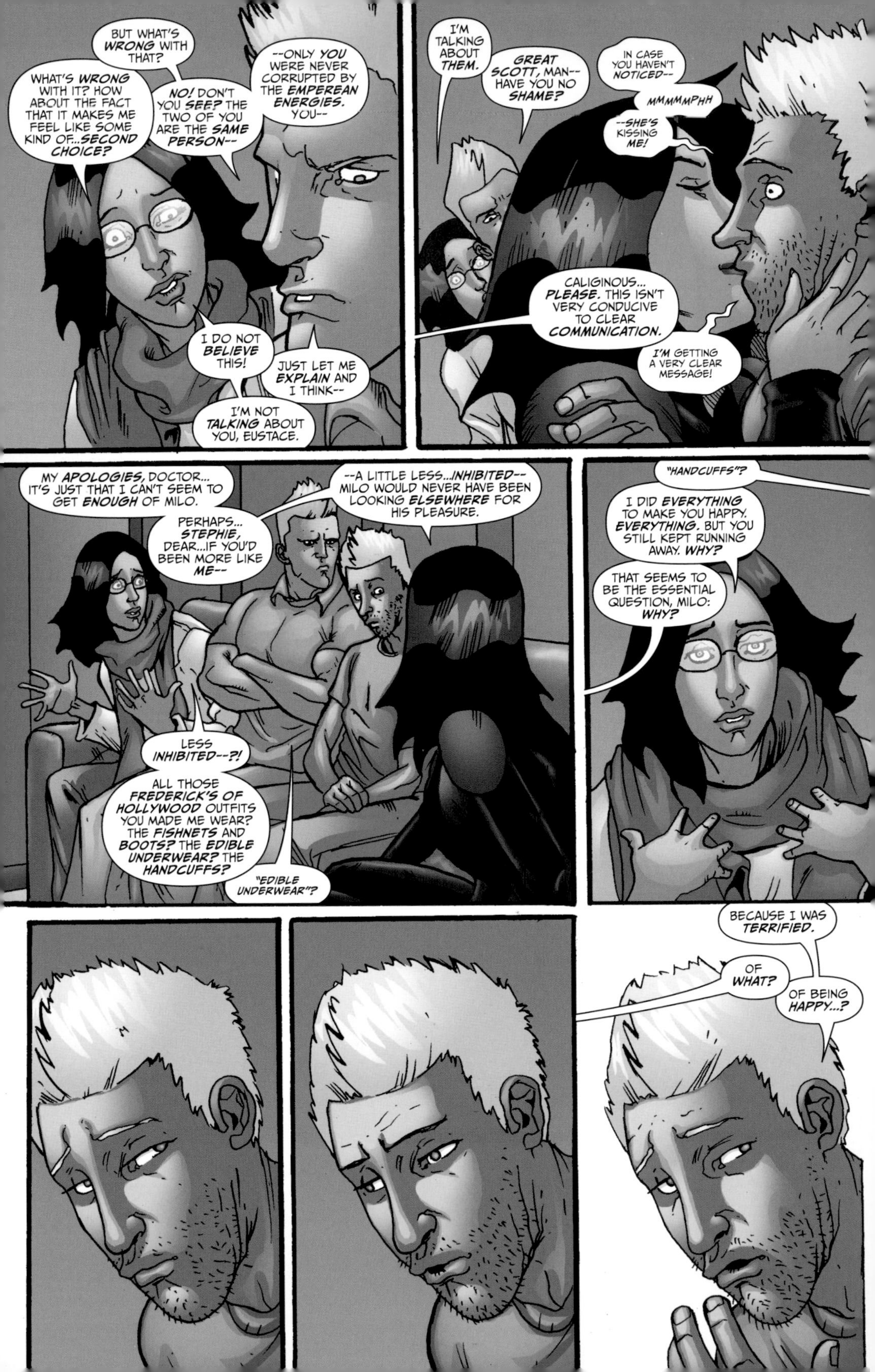
BUT WHAT'S WRONG WITH THAT?
WHAT'S WRONG WITH IT? HOW ABOUT THE FACT THAT IT MAKES ME FEEL LIKE SOME KIND OF...SECOND CHOICE?
NO! DON'T YOU SEE? THE TWO OF YOU ARE THE SAME PERSON--
--ONLY YOU WERE NEVER CORRUPTED BY THE EMPEREAN ENERGIES. YOU--
I DO NOT BELIEVE THIS!
JUST LET ME EXPLAIN AND I THINK--
I'M NOT TALKING ABOUT YOU, EUSTACE.
I'M TALKING ABOUT THEM.
GREAT SCOTT, MAN--HAVE YOU NO SHAME?
IN CASE YOU HAVEN'T NOTICED--
MMMMMPHH
--SHE'S KISSING ME!
CALIGINOUS... PLEASE. THIS ISN'T VERY CONDUCIVE TO CLEAR COMMUNICATION.
I'M GETTING A VERY CLEAR MESSAGE!
MY APOLOGIES, DOCTOR... IT'S JUST THAT I CAN'T SEEM TO GET ENOUGH OF MILO.
PERHAPS... STEPHIE, DEAR...IF YOU'D BEEN MORE LIKE ME--
--A LITTLE LESS...INHIBITED--MILO WOULD NEVER HAVE BEEN LOOKING ELSEWHERE FOR HIS PLEASURE.
LESS INHIBITED--?!
ALL THOSE FREDERICK'S OF HOLLYWOOD OUTFITS YOU MADE ME WEAR? THE FISHNETS AND BOOTS? THE EDIBLE UNDERWEAR? THE HANDCUFFS?
"EDIBLE UNDERWEAR"?
"HANDCUFFS"?
I DID EVERYTHING TO MAKE YOU HAPPY. EVERYTHING. BUT YOU STILL KEPT RUNNING AWAY. WHY?
THAT SEEMS TO BE THE ESSENTIAL QUESTION, MILO: WHY?
BECAUSE I WAS TERRIFIED.
OF WHAT?
OF BEING HAPPY...?

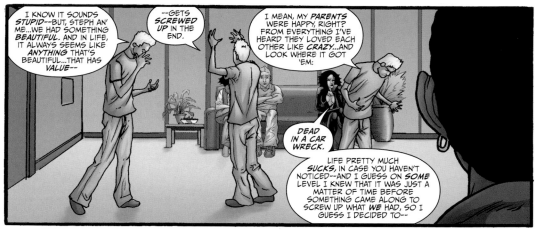

I KNOW IT SOUNDS STUPID--BUT, STEPH AN' ME...WE HAD SOMETHING BEAUTIFUL. AND IN LIFE, IT ALWAYS SEEMS LIKE ANYTHING THAT'S BEAUTIFUL...THAT HAS VALUE--

--GETS SCREWED UP IN THE END.

I MEAN, MY PARENTS WERE HAPPY, RIGHT? FROM EVERYTHING I'VE HEARD THEY LOVED EACH OTHER LIKE CRAZY...AND LOOK WHERE IT GOT 'EM:

DEAD IN A CAR WRECK.

LIFE PRETTY MUCH SUCKS, IN CASE YOU HAVEN'T NOTICED--AND I GUESS ON SOME LEVEL I KNEW THAT IT WAS JUST A MATTER OF TIME BEFORE SOMETHING CAME ALONG TO SCREW UP WHAT WE HAD, SO I GUESS I DECIDED TO--

DECIDED TO WHAT?

I DUNNO. I'M JUST BABBLING, I--

DECIDED TO WHAT, MILO?

-:SIGH:- TO SCREW US UP FIRST--

--AND SAVE MYSELF THE HEARTACHE.

BUT WHAT ABOUT ME?

WHAT ABOUT MY HEARTACHE?

YOU'RE A SURVIVOR, STEPH. ALWAYS HAVE BEEN. NOTHING CAN STOP YOU.

C'MON, LET'S FACE IT: YOU WERE ALWAYS TAKING CARE OF ME. I WAS MORE LIKE YOUR KID THAN YOUR BOYFRIEND.

IT'S NOT LIKE YOU EVER REALLY NEEDED ME.

BUT I COULD TAKE CARE OF HER.

I MEAN, YEAH-- SHE'S GOT THE BAD-GIRL THING DOWN...AND SHE HAS THIS TRICK SHE DOES WITH HER THIGHS AND TWO ANTIGRAVITY DISCS THAT'S NOT TO BE BELIEVED--

--BUT THERE'S MORE TO HER THAN THAT. UNDERNEATH IT ALL--SHE'S HURTING. SHE'S--

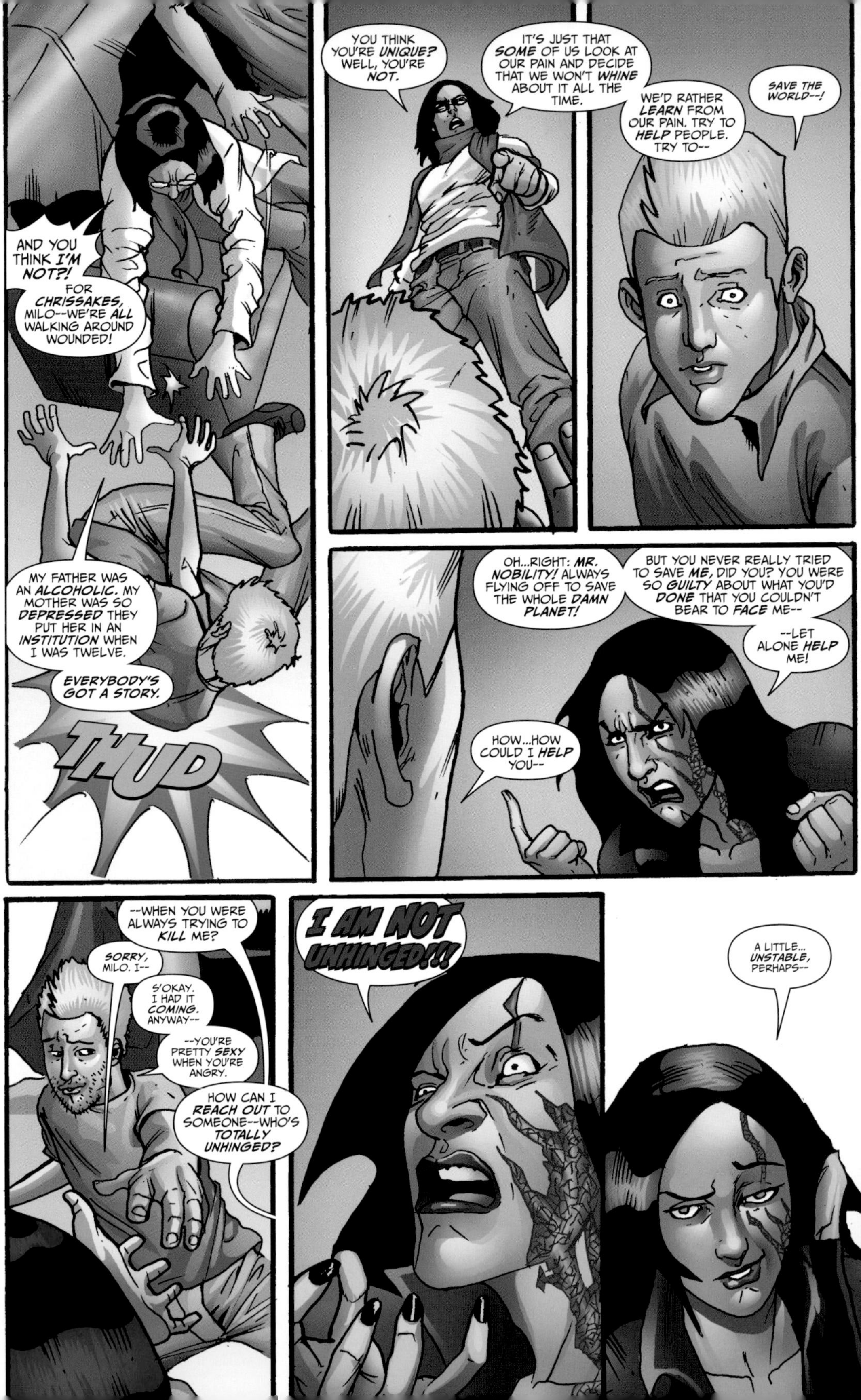
AND YOU THINK I'M NOT?!
FOR CHRISSAKES, MILO--WE'RE ALL WALKING AROUND WOUNDED!
MY FATHER WAS AN ALCOHOLIC. MY MOTHER WAS SO DEPRESSED THEY PUT HER IN AN INSTITUTION WHEN I WAS TWELVE.
EVERYBODY'S GOT A STORY.
THUD
YOU THINK YOU'RE UNIQUE? WELL, YOU'RE NOT.
IT'S JUST THAT SOME OF US LOOK AT OUR PAIN AND DECIDE THAT WE WON'T WHINE ABOUT IT ALL THE TIME.
WE'D RATHER LEARN FROM OUR PAIN. TRY TO HELP PEOPLE. TRY TO--
SAVE THE WORLD--!
OH...RIGHT: MR. NOBILITY! ALWAYS FLYING OFF TO SAVE THE WHOLE DAMN PLANET!
BUT YOU NEVER REALLY TRIED TO SAVE ME, DID YOU? YOU WERE SO GUILTY ABOUT WHAT YOU'D DONE THAT YOU COULDN'T BEAR TO FACE ME--
--LET ALONE HELP ME!
HOW...HOW COULD I HELP YOU--
--WHEN YOU WERE ALWAYS TRYING TO KILL ME?
SORRY, MILO. I--
S'OKAY. I HAD IT COMING. ANYWAY--
--YOU'RE PRETTY SEXY WHEN YOU'RE ANGRY.
HOW CAN I REACH OUT TO SOMEONE--WHO'S TOTALLY UNHINGED?
I AM NOT UNHINGED!!!
A LITTLE... UNSTABLE, PERHAPS--

THE NECTAR... FROM THE *CHALICE*-- WHEN IT SPILLED *OVER* ME...BURNED *THROUGH* ME--

--THE ENERGY WAS *OVERWHELMING.* IT'S *STILL* OVERWHELMING.

SOMETIMES... SOMETIMES IT FEELS LIKE IT'S THE *ENERGY ITSELF* THINKING...ACTING. LIKE IT'S NOT *ME* AT ALL.

SOMETIMES I CAN'T TELL WHERE THE *EMPYREAN POWER* LEAVES OFF--

--AND *I* BEGIN.

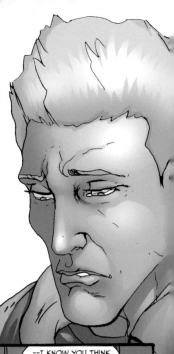

CALIGINOUS--

--STEPHIE--

--I KNOW YOU THINK I'M TO *BLAME* FOR ALL THIS--AND...IN SOME WAYS...I GUESS I *AM*--

--BUT YOU *HAVE* TO BELIEVE THAT I NEVER MEANT IT TO *BE* THIS WAY.

YOU...YOU MIGHT BE *RIGHT.* MAYBE...ON SOME LEVEL...SEEING YOU AS A VILLAIN WAS A CONVENIENT WAY FOR ME TO *SIDESTEP* MY GUILT.

BUT IF THAT'S THE CASE...IT WASN'T *CONSCIOUS.* I DIDN'T *TRY* TO DO THAT...IT JUST--

--IT JUST *HAPPENED.*

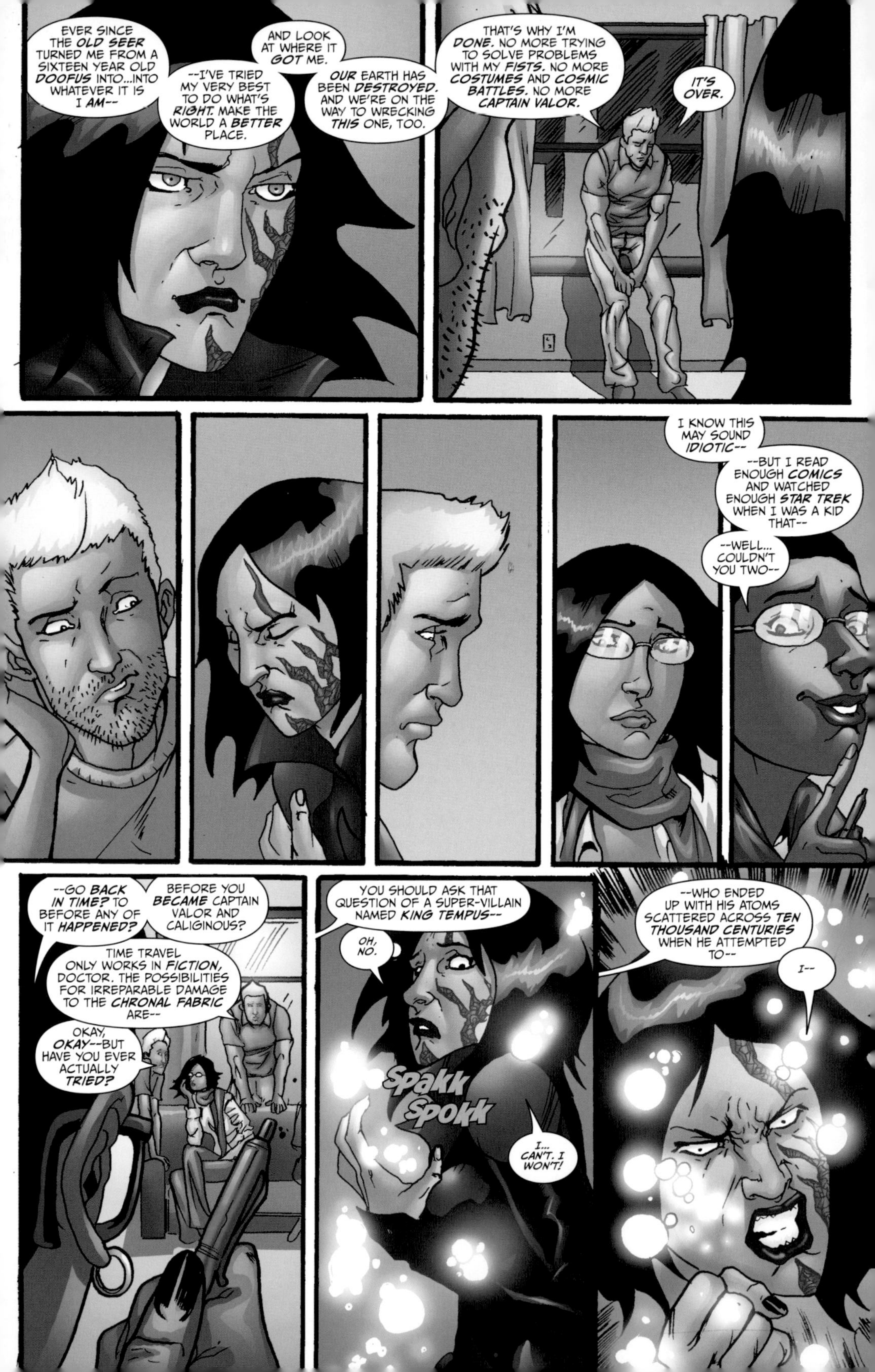
EVER SINCE THE OLD SEER TURNED ME FROM A SIXTEEN YEAR OLD DOOFUS INTO...INTO WHATEVER IT IS I AM--
--I'VE TRIED MY VERY BEST TO DO WHAT'S RIGHT. MAKE THE WORLD A BETTER PLACE.
AND LOOK AT WHERE IT GOT ME.
OUR EARTH HAS BEEN DESTROYED. AND WE'RE ON THE WAY TO WRECKING THIS ONE, TOO.
THAT'S WHY I'M DONE. NO MORE TRYING TO SOLVE PROBLEMS WITH MY FISTS. NO MORE COSTUMES AND COSMIC BATTLES. NO MORE CAPTAIN VALOR.
IT'S OVER.
I KNOW THIS MAY SOUND IDIOTIC--
--BUT I READ ENOUGH COMICS AND WATCHED ENOUGH STAR TREK WHEN I WAS A KID THAT--
--WELL... COULDN'T YOU TWO--
--GO BACK IN TIME? TO BEFORE ANY OF IT HAPPENED?
BEFORE YOU BECAME CAPTAIN VALOR AND CALIGINOUS?
TIME TRAVEL ONLY WORKS IN FICTION, DOCTOR. THE POSSIBILITIES FOR IRREPARABLE DAMAGE TO THE CHRONAL FABRIC ARE--
OKAY, OKAY--BUT HAVE YOU EVER ACTUALLY TRIED?
YOU SHOULD ASK THAT QUESTION OF A SUPER-VILLAIN NAMED KING TEMPUS--
OH, NO.
Spakk
Spokk
I... CAN'T. I WON'T!
--WHO ENDED UP WITH HIS ATOMS SCATTERED ACROSS TEN THOUSAND CENTURIES WHEN HE ATTEMPTED TO--
I--

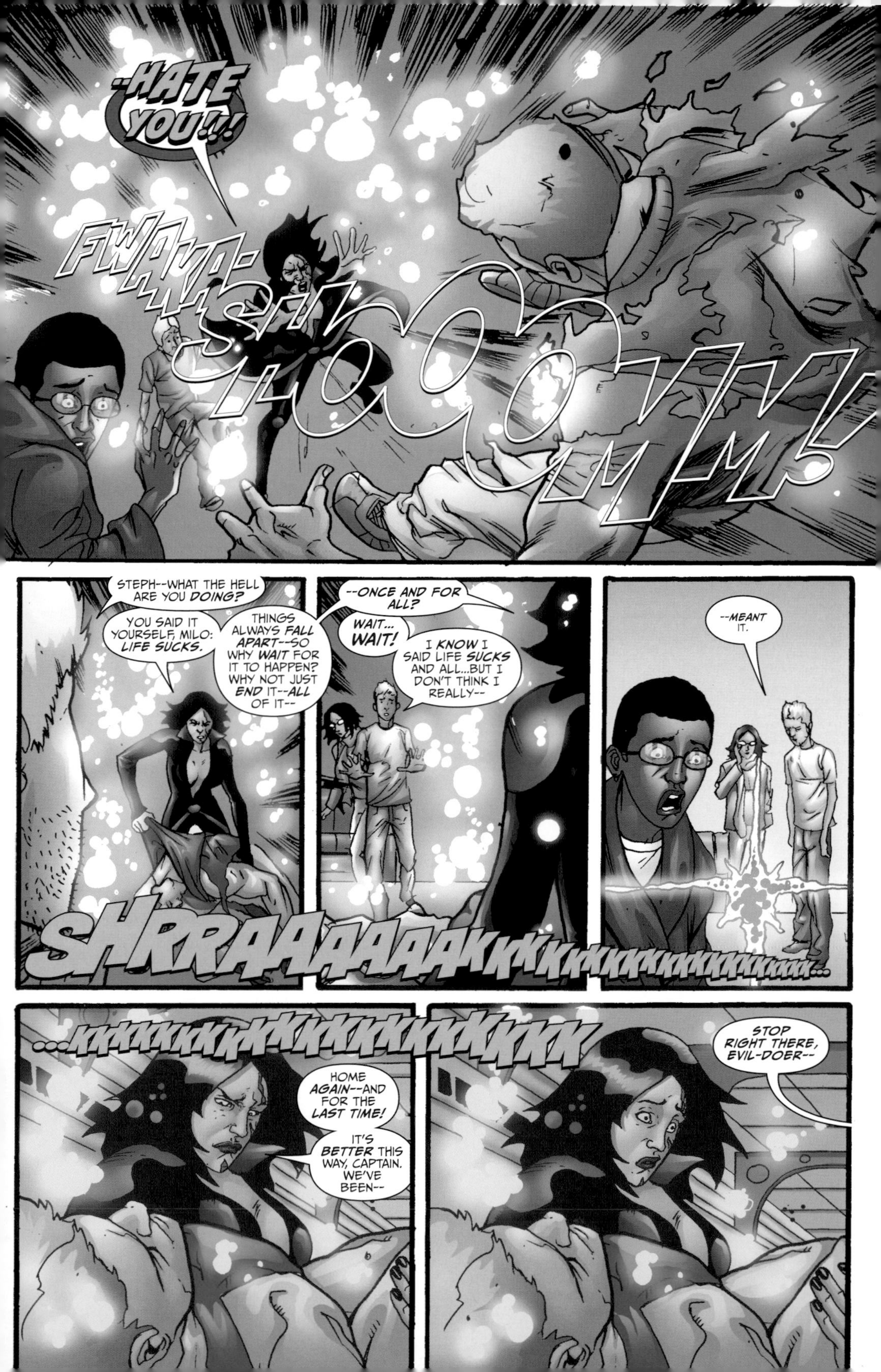
--HATE YOU!!!
FWAKA-SHOOOOOMMM!
STEPH--WHAT THE HELL ARE YOU DOING?
YOU SAID IT YOURSELF, MILO: LIFE SUCKS.
THINGS ALWAYS FALL APART--SO WHY WAIT FOR IT TO HAPPEN? WHY NOT JUST END IT--ALL OF IT--
--ONCE AND FOR ALL?
WAIT... WAIT!
I KNOW I SAID LIFE SUCKS AND ALL...BUT I DON'T THINK I REALLY--
--MEANT IT.
SHRRAAAAAAAKKKKKKKKKKKKKKKKKK...
...KKKKKKKKKKKKKKKKKKKKKKKKK
HOME AGAIN--AND FOR THE LAST TIME!
IT'S BETTER THIS WAY, CAPTAIN. WE'VE BEEN--
STOP RIGHT THERE, EVIL-DOER--

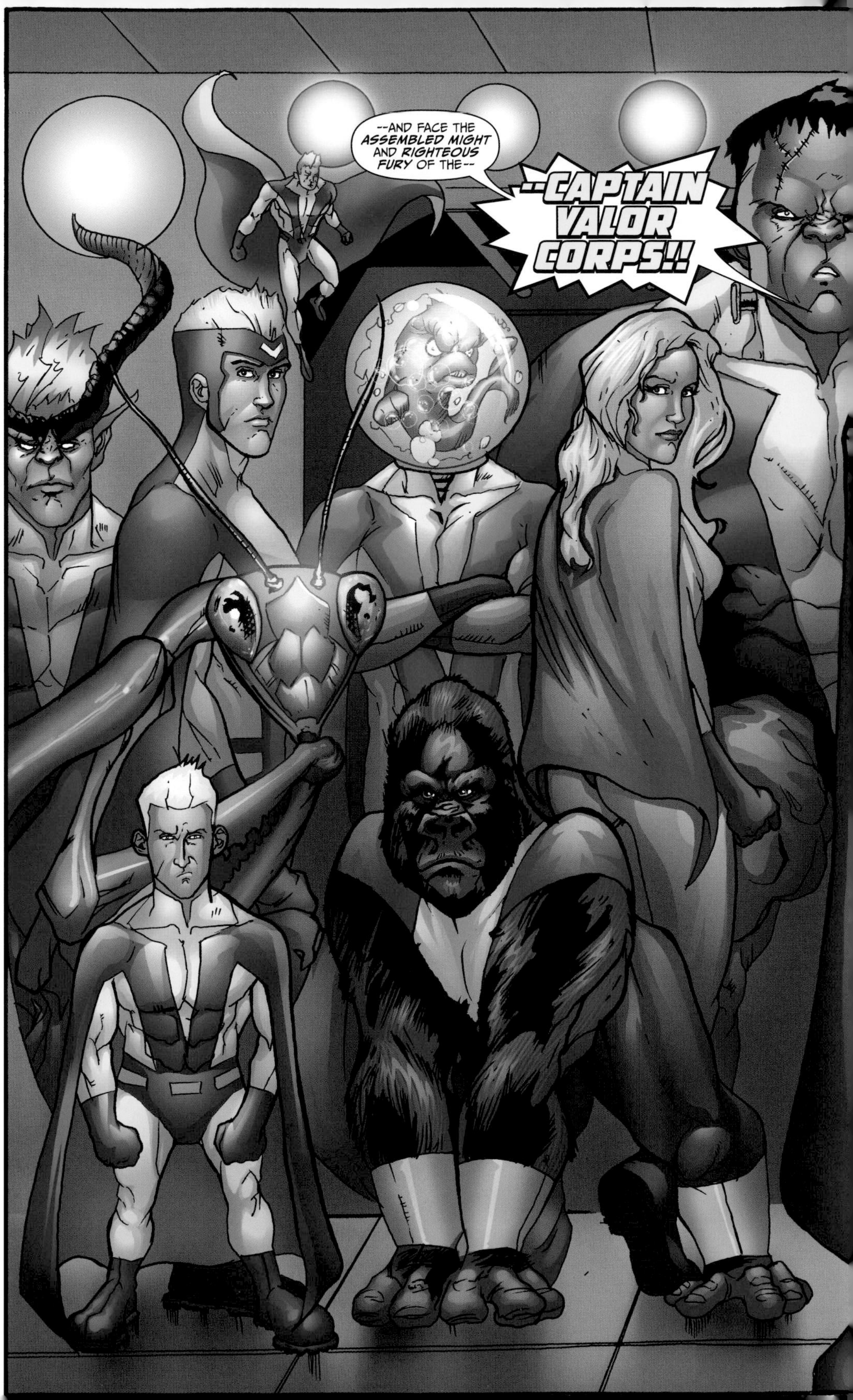
--AND FACE THE ASSEMBLED MIGHT AND RIGHTEOUS FURY OF THE--
--CAPTAIN VALOR CORPS!!

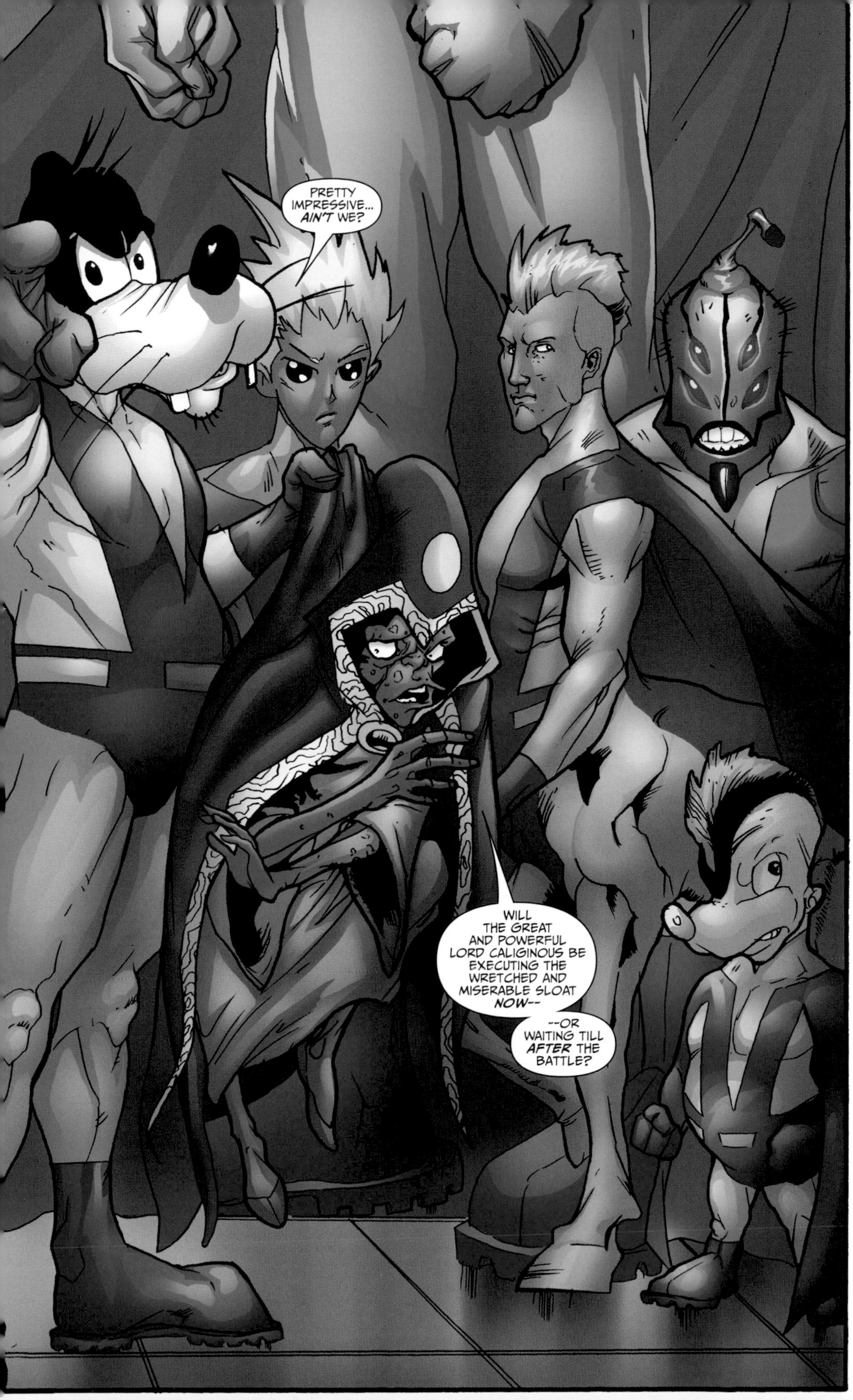
PRETTY IMPRESSIVE... AIN'T WE?
WILL THE GREAT AND POWERFUL LORD CALIGINOUS BE EXECUTING THE WRETCHED AND MISERABLE SLOAT NOW--
--OR WAITING TILL AFTER THE BATTLE?

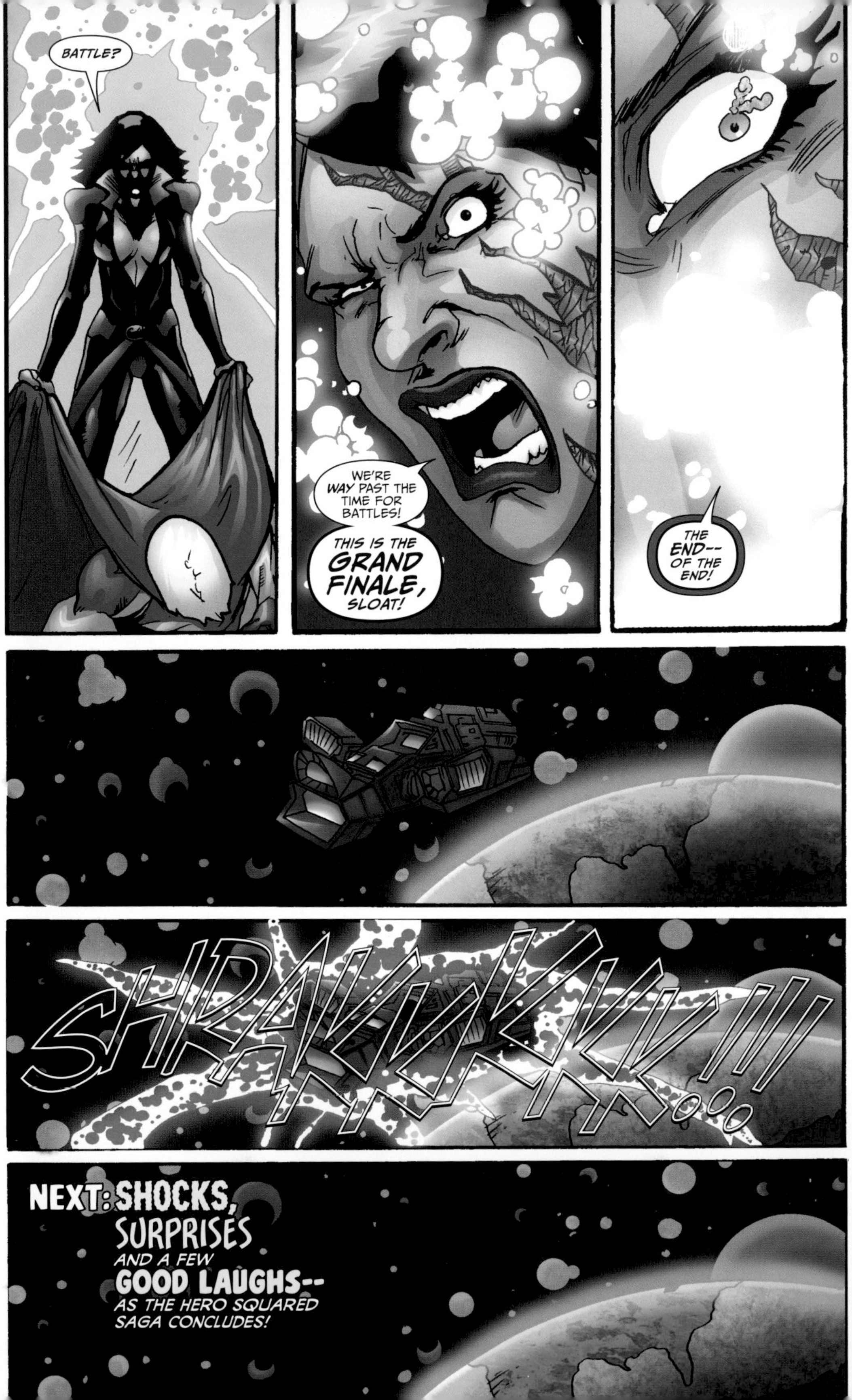
BATTLE?
WE'RE WAY PAST THE TIME FOR BATTLES!
THIS IS THE GRAND FINALE, SLOAT!
THE END-- OF THE END!
SHRAKKKKKKK!!!
NEXT: SHOCKS, SURPRISES AND A FEW GOOD LAUGHS-- AS THE HERO SQUARED SAGA CONCLUDES!

CHAPTER 3

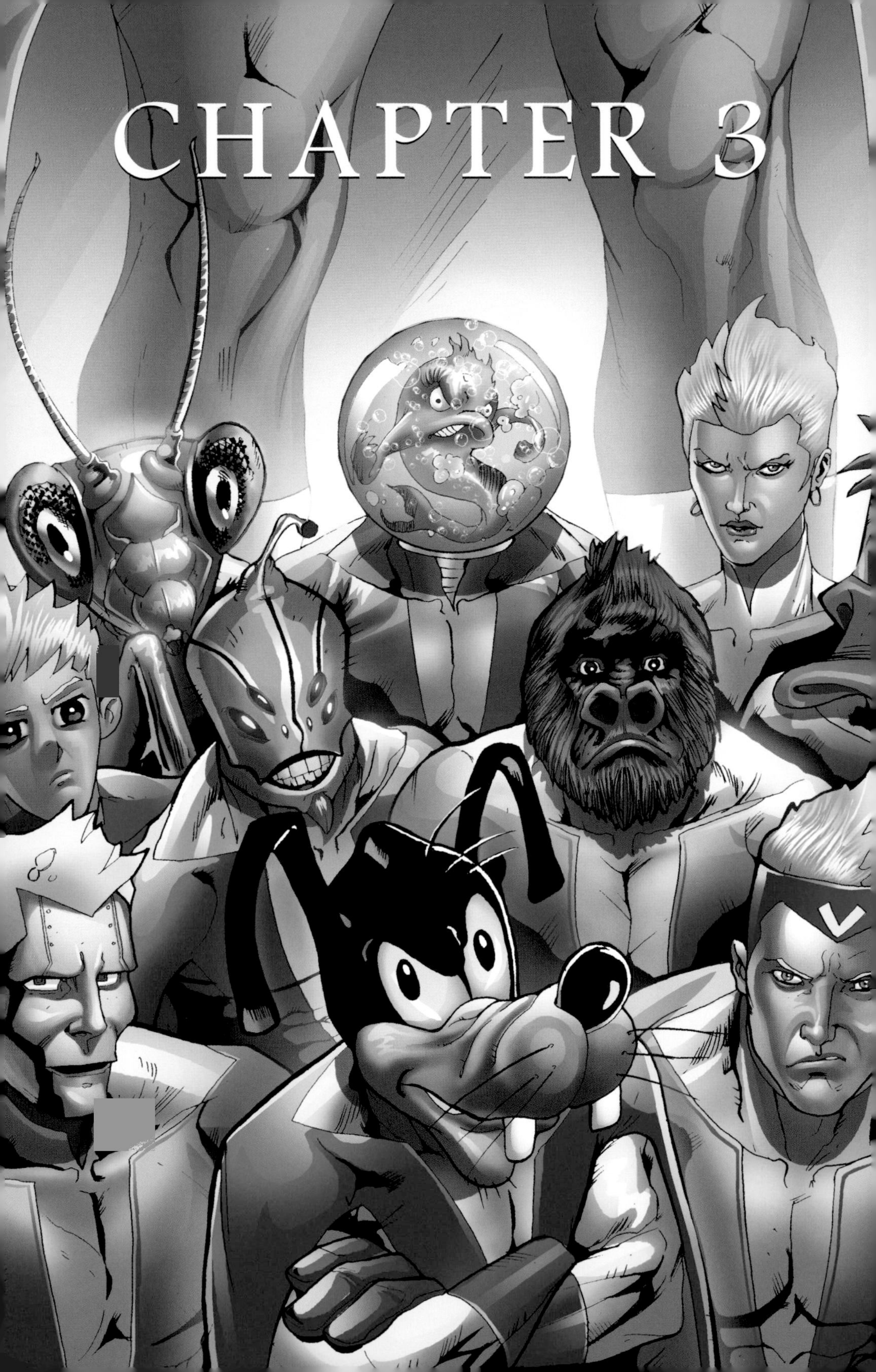

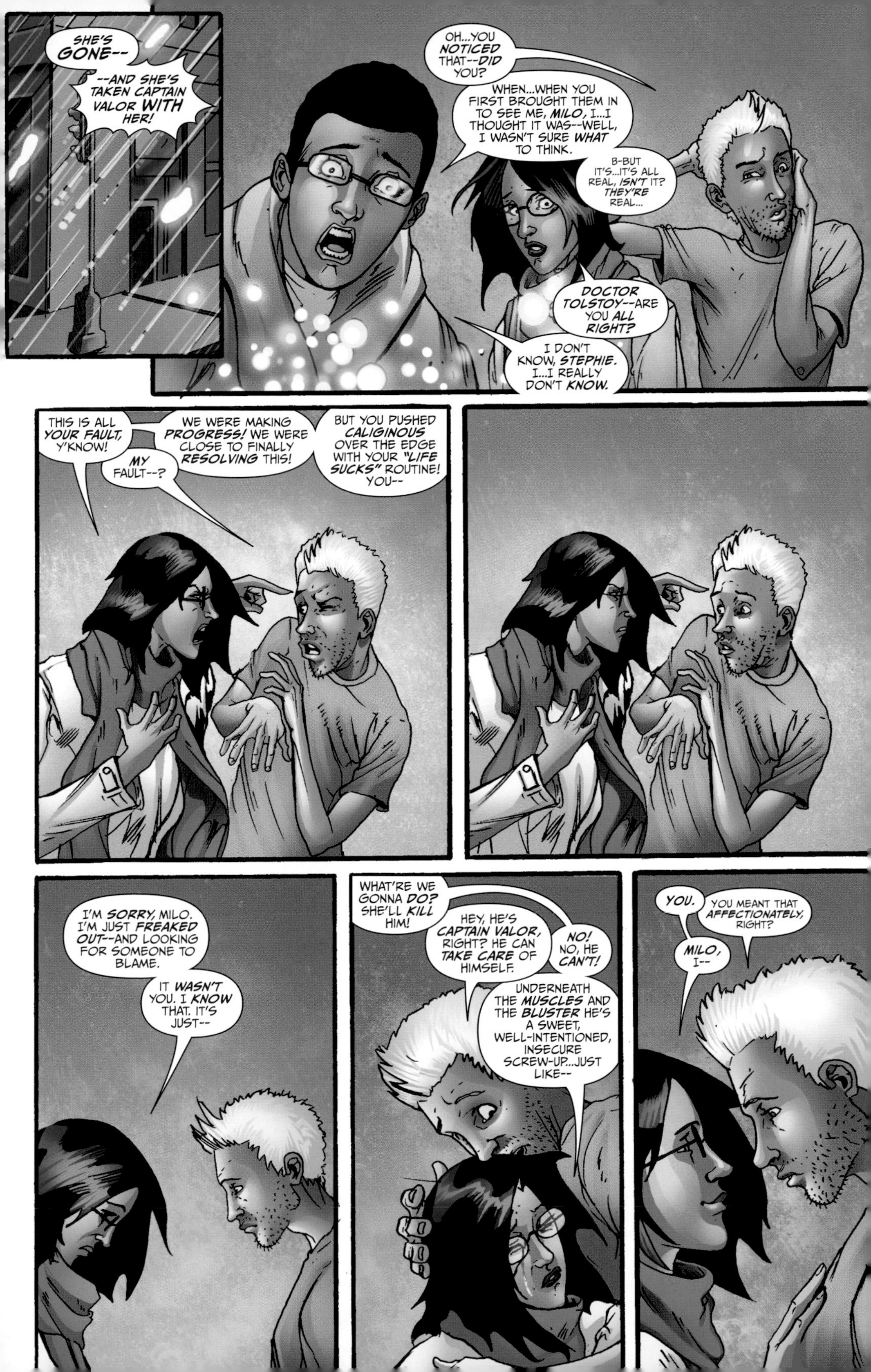
SHE'S GONE--
--AND SHE'S TAKEN CAPTAIN VALOR WITH HER!
OH...YOU NOTICED THAT--DID YOU?
WHEN...WHEN YOU FIRST BROUGHT THEM IN TO SEE ME, MILO, I...I THOUGHT IT WAS--WELL, I WASN'T SURE WHAT TO THINK.
B-BUT IT'S...IT'S ALL REAL, ISN'T IT? THEY'RE REAL...
DOCTOR TOLSTOY--ARE YOU ALL RIGHT?
I DON'T KNOW, STEPHIE. I...I REALLY DON'T KNOW.
THIS IS ALL YOUR FAULT, Y'KNOW!
MY FAULT--?
WE WERE MAKING PROGRESS! WE WERE CLOSE TO FINALLY RESOLVING THIS!
BUT YOU PUSHED CALIGINOUS OVER THE EDGE WITH YOUR "LIFE SUCKS" ROUTINE! YOU--
I'M SORRY, MILO. I'M JUST FREAKED OUT--AND LOOKING FOR SOMEONE TO BLAME.
IT WASN'T YOU. I KNOW THAT. IT'S JUST--
WHAT'RE WE GONNA DO? SHE'LL KILL HIM!
HEY, HE'S CAPTAIN VALOR, RIGHT? HE CAN TAKE CARE OF HIMSELF.
NO! NO, HE CAN'T!
UNDERNEATH THE MUSCLES AND THE BLUSTER HE'S A SWEET, WELL-INTENTIONED, INSECURE SCREW-UP...JUST LIKE--
YOU.
YOU MEANT THAT AFFECTIONATELY, RIGHT?
MILO, I--

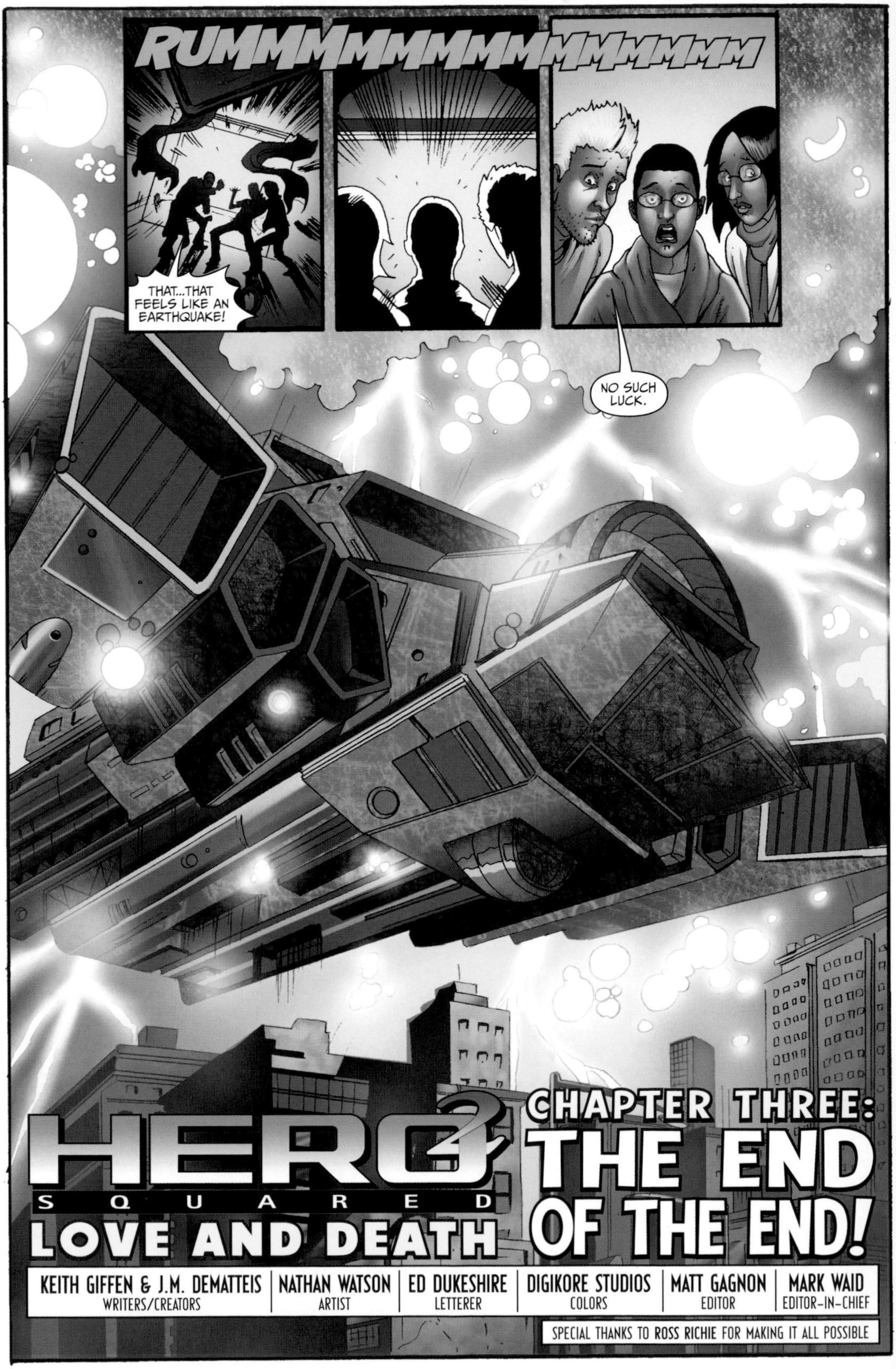

RUMMMMMMMMMMMMMMMM
THAT...THAT FEELS LIKE AN EARTHQUAKE!
NO SUCH LUCK.
HERO SQUARED
LOVE AND DEATH
CHAPTER THREE: THE END OF THE END!
KEITH GIFFEN & J.M. DEMATTEIS WRITERS/CREATORS
NATHAN WATSON ARTIST
ED DUKESHIRE LETTERER
DIGIKORE STUDIOS COLORS
MATT GAGNON EDITOR
MARK WAID EDITOR-IN-CHIEF
SPECIAL THANKS TO ROSS RICHIE FOR MAKING IT ALL POSSIBLE

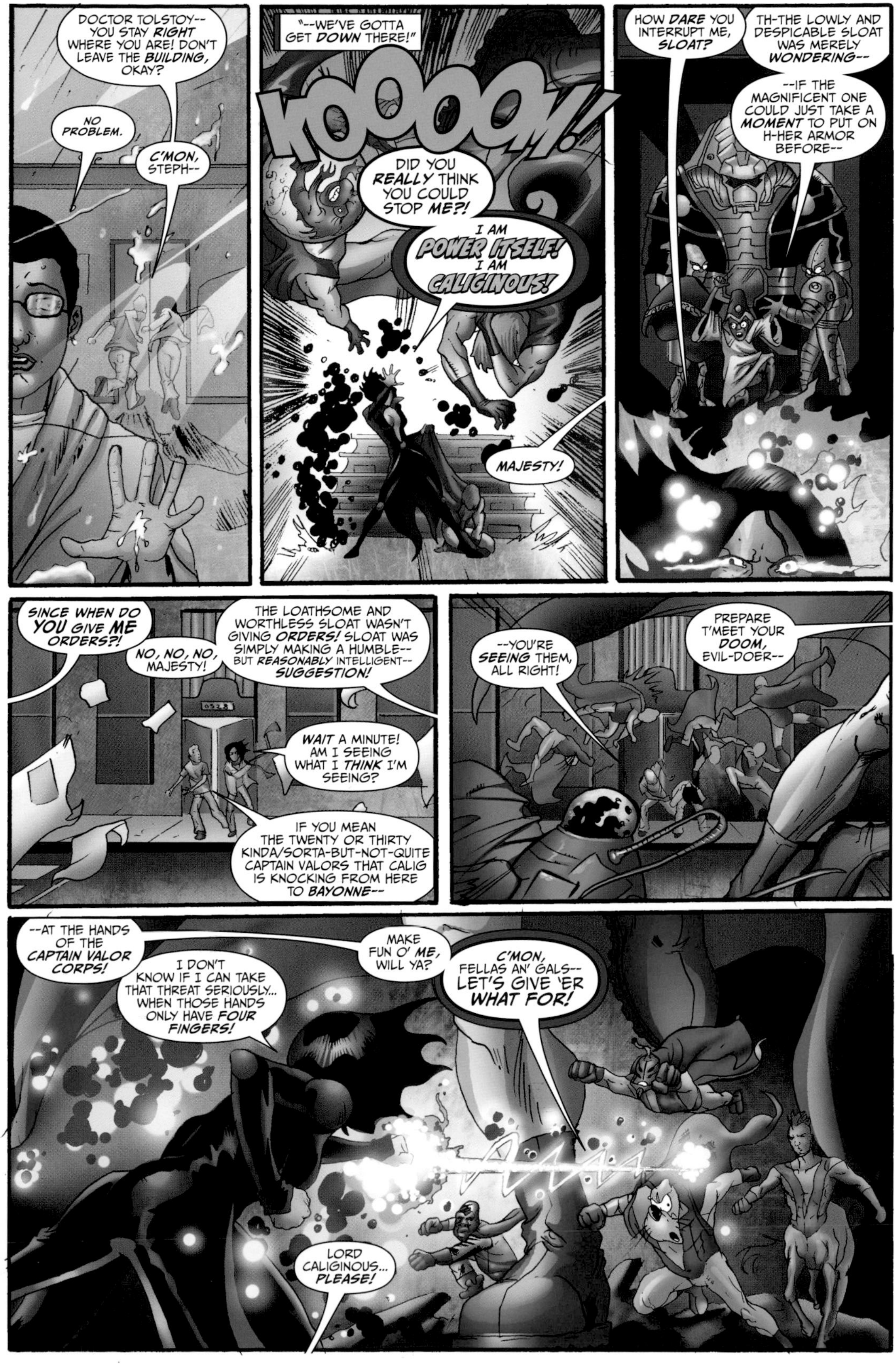
DOCTOR TOLSTOY-- YOU STAY RIGHT WHERE YOU ARE! DON'T LEAVE THE BUILDING, OKAY?
NO PROBLEM.
C'MON, STEPH--
"--WE'VE GOTTA GET DOWN THERE!"
KOOOOM!
DID YOU REALLY THINK YOU COULD STOP ME?!
I AM POWER ITSELF! I AM CALIGINOUS!
MAJESTY!
HOW DARE YOU INTERRUPT ME, SLOAT?
TH-THE LOWLY AND DESPICABLE SLOAT WAS MERELY WONDERING--
--IF THE MAGNIFICENT ONE COULD JUST TAKE A MOMENT TO PUT ON H-HER ARMOR BEFORE--
SINCE WHEN DO YOU GIVE ME ORDERS?!
NO, NO, NO, MAJESTY!
THE LOATHSOME AND WORTHLESS SLOAT WASN'T GIVING ORDERS! SLOAT WAS SIMPLY MAKING A HUMBLE-- BUT REASONABLY INTELLIGENT-- SUGGESTION!
0528
WAIT A MINUTE! AM I SEEING WHAT I THINK I'M SEEING?
IF YOU MEAN THE TWENTY OR THIRTY KINDA/SORTA-BUT-NOT-QUITE CAPTAIN VALORS THAT CALIG IS KNOCKING FROM HERE TO BAYONNE--
--YOU'RE SEEING THEM, ALL RIGHT!
PREPARE T'MEET YOUR DOOM, EVIL-DOER--
--AT THE HANDS OF THE CAPTAIN VALOR CORPS!
I DON'T KNOW IF I CAN TAKE THAT THREAT SERIOUSLY... WHEN THOSE HANDS ONLY HAVE FOUR FINGERS!
MAKE FUN O' ME, WILL YA?
C'MON, FELLAS AN' GALS-- LET'S GIVE 'ER WHAT FOR!
LORD CALIGINOUS... PLEASE!

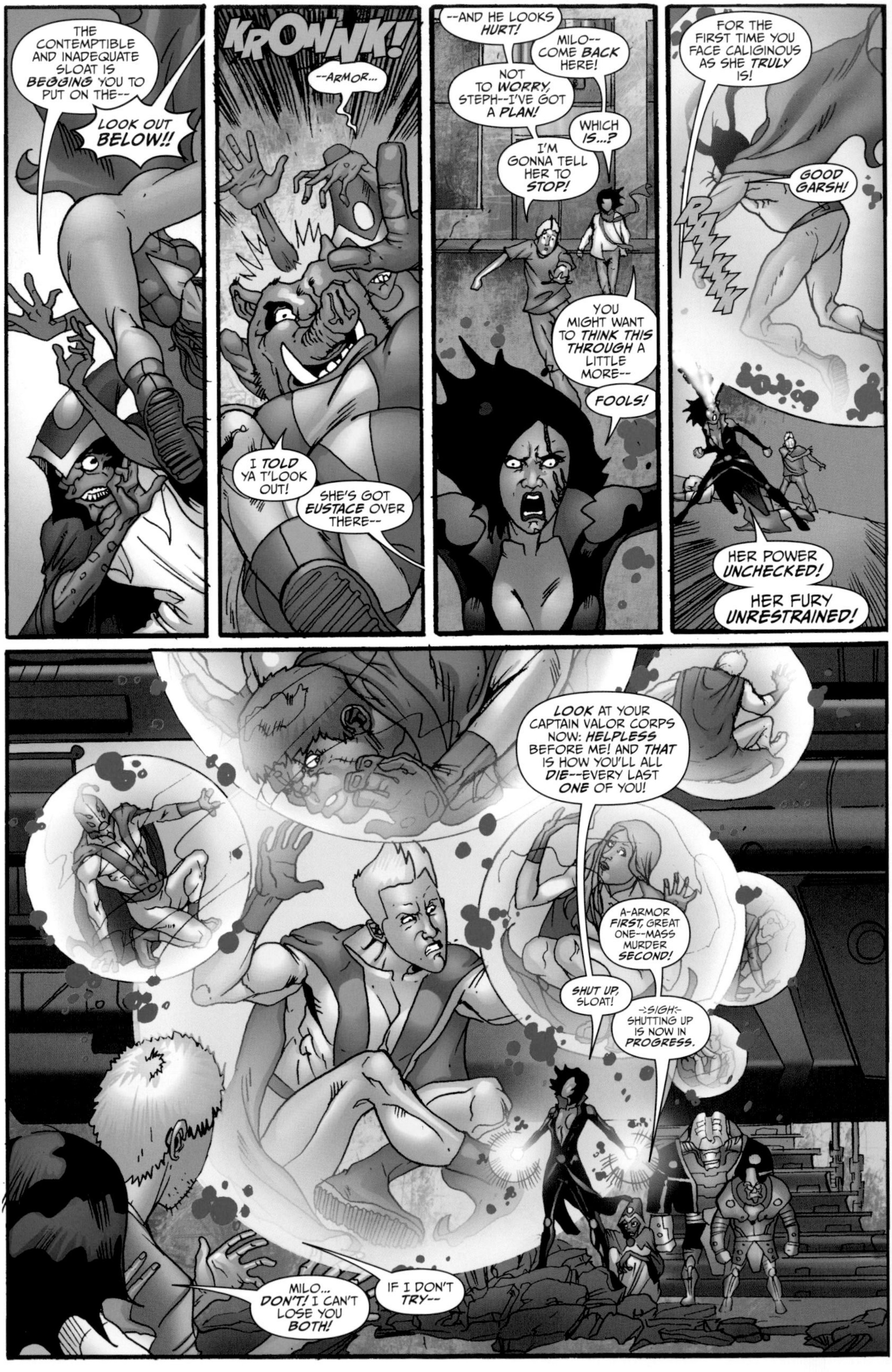
THE CONTEMPTIBLE AND INADEQUATE SLOAT IS BEGGING YOU TO PUT ON THE--
LOOK OUT BELOW!!
KRONNK!
--ARMOR...
I TOLD YA T'LOOK OUT!
SHE'S GOT EUSTACE OVER THERE--
--AND HE LOOKS HURT!
MILO--COME BACK HERE!
NOT TO WORRY, STEPH--I'VE GOT A PLAN!
WHICH IS...?
I'M GONNA TELL HER TO STOP!
YOU MIGHT WANT TO THINK THIS THROUGH A LITTLE MORE--
FOOLS!
FOR THE FIRST TIME YOU FACE CALIGINOUS AS SHE TRULY IS!
GOOD GARSH!
RAKKK
HER POWER UNCHECKED!
HER FURY UNRESTRAINED!
LOOK AT YOUR CAPTAIN VALOR CORPS NOW: HELPLESS BEFORE ME! AND THAT IS HOW YOU'LL ALL DIE--EVERY LAST ONE OF YOU!
A-ARMOR FIRST, GREAT ONE--MASS MURDER SECOND!
SHUT UP, SLOAT!
-SIGH- SHUTTING UP IS NOW IN PROGRESS.
MILO... DON'T! I CAN'T LOSE YOU BOTH!
IF I DON'T TRY--

--THIS WHOLE CITY'S LOST!

CALIGINOUS...LISTEN TO ME! YOU DON'T WANNA DO THIS!

ACTUALLY... I DO!

IN DOCTOR TOLSTOY'S OFFICE YOU SAID THAT SOMETIMES THE EMPYREAN ENERGIES...THEY TAKE CONTROL OF YOU!

I THINK THAT'S WHAT'S HAPPENING NOW! BUT YOU CAN FIGHT IT...I KNOW YOU CAN!

IMBECILE! YOU DON'T KNOW ANYTHING! YOU--

IMBECILE...?

MILO...?

MILO, DARLING--IS THAT YOU?

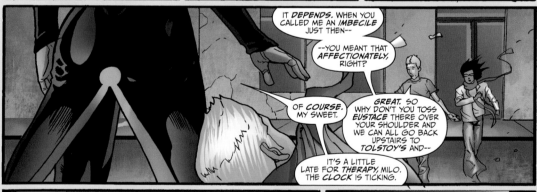

IT DEPENDS. WHEN YOU CALLED ME AN IMBECILE JUST THEN--

--YOU MEANT THAT AFFECTIONATELY, RIGHT?

OF COURSE. MY SWEET.

GREAT. SO WHY DON'T YOU TOSS EUSTACE THERE OVER YOUR SHOULDER AND WE CAN ALL GO BACK UPSTAIRS TO TOLSTOY'S AND--

IT'S A LITTLE LATE FOR THERAPY, MILO. THE CLOCK IS TICKING.

CLOCK...?

THE DOOMSDAY CLOCK.

DOOMSDAY AS IN--THE END OF THE WORLD?

DOOMSDAY AS IN--THE END OF ALL WORLDS.

AN ENDING THAT WAS WRITTEN-- THE MOMENT CAPTAIN VALOR... MY CAPTAIN VALOR... AND I SET FOOT ON THIS PLANET.

I'M NOT FOLLOWING YOU--

WHEN WE FIRST PHASED FROM OUR EARTH TO YOURS... WE INADVERTENTLY CREATED A SMALL TEAR IN THE INTER-DIMENSIONAL FABRIC--

CAN'T YOU JUST TAKE IT TO AN INTER-DIMENSIONAL TAILOR?

MILO--!

SORRY.

--AND THAT TEAR HAS BEEN GROWING WIDER EVER SINCE--

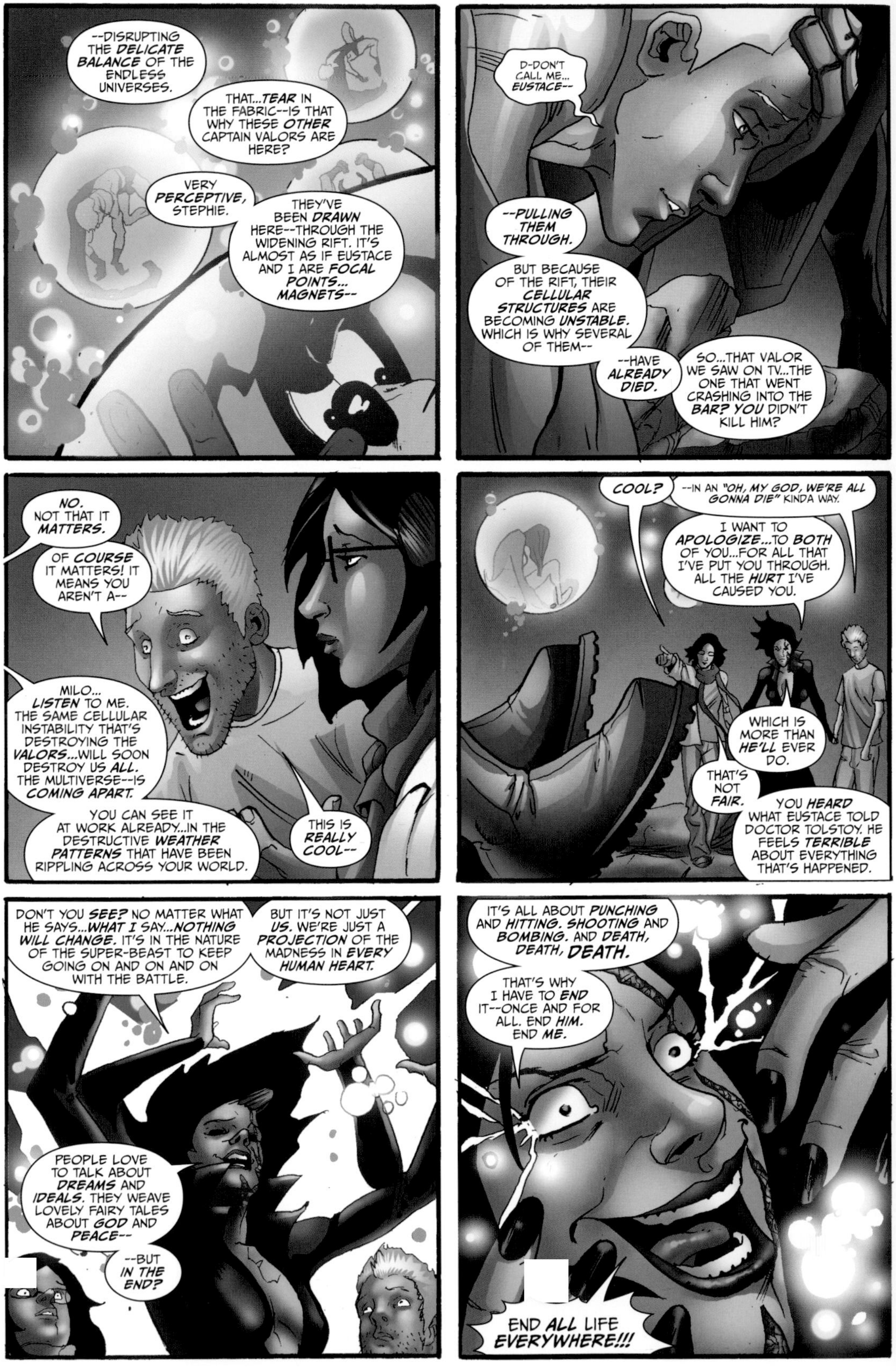
--DISRUPTING THE DELICATE BALANCE OF THE ENDLESS UNIVERSES.
THAT...TEAR IN THE FABRIC--IS THAT WHY THESE OTHER CAPTAIN VALORS ARE HERE?
VERY PERCEPTIVE, STEPHIE.
THEY'VE BEEN DRAWN HERE--THROUGH THE WIDENING RIFT. IT'S ALMOST AS IF EUSTACE AND I ARE FOCAL POINTS... MAGNETS--
D-DON'T CALL ME... EUSTACE--
--PULLING THEM THROUGH.
BUT BECAUSE OF THE RIFT, THEIR CELLULAR STRUCTURES ARE BECOMING UNSTABLE. WHICH IS WHY SEVERAL OF THEM--
--HAVE ALREADY DIED.
SO...THAT VALOR WE SAW ON TV...THE ONE THAT WENT CRASHING INTO THE BAR? YOU DIDN'T KILL HIM?
NO. NOT THAT IT MATTERS.
OF COURSE IT MATTERS! IT MEANS YOU AREN'T A--
MILO... LISTEN TO ME. THE SAME CELLULAR INSTABILITY THAT'S DESTROYING THE VALORS...WILL SOON DESTROY US ALL. THE MULTIVERSE--IS COMING APART.
YOU CAN SEE IT AT WORK ALREADY...IN THE DESTRUCTIVE WEATHER PATTERNS THAT HAVE BEEN RIPPLING ACROSS YOUR WORLD.
THIS IS REALLY COOL--
COOL?
--IN AN "OH, MY GOD, WE'RE ALL GONNA DIE" KINDA WAY.
I WANT TO APOLOGIZE...TO BOTH OF YOU...FOR ALL THAT I'VE PUT YOU THROUGH. ALL THE HURT I'VE CAUSED YOU.
WHICH IS MORE THAN HE'LL EVER DO.
THAT'S NOT FAIR.
YOU HEARD WHAT EUSTACE TOLD DOCTOR TOLSTOY. HE FEELS TERRIBLE ABOUT EVERYTHING THAT'S HAPPENED.
DON'T YOU SEE? NO MATTER WHAT HE SAYS...WHAT I SAY...NOTHING WILL CHANGE. IT'S IN THE NATURE OF THE SUPER-BEAST TO KEEP GOING ON AND ON AND ON WITH THE BATTLE.
BUT IT'S NOT JUST US. WE'RE JUST A PROJECTION OF THE MADNESS IN EVERY HUMAN HEART.
PEOPLE LOVE TO TALK ABOUT DREAMS AND IDEALS. THEY WEAVE LOVELY FAIRY TALES ABOUT GOD AND PEACE--
--BUT IN THE END?
IT'S ALL ABOUT PUNCHING AND HITTING. SHOOTING AND BOMBING. AND DEATH, DEATH, DEATH.
THAT'S WHY I HAVE TO END IT--ONCE AND FOR ALL. END HIM. END ME.
END ALL LIFE EVERYWHERE!!!

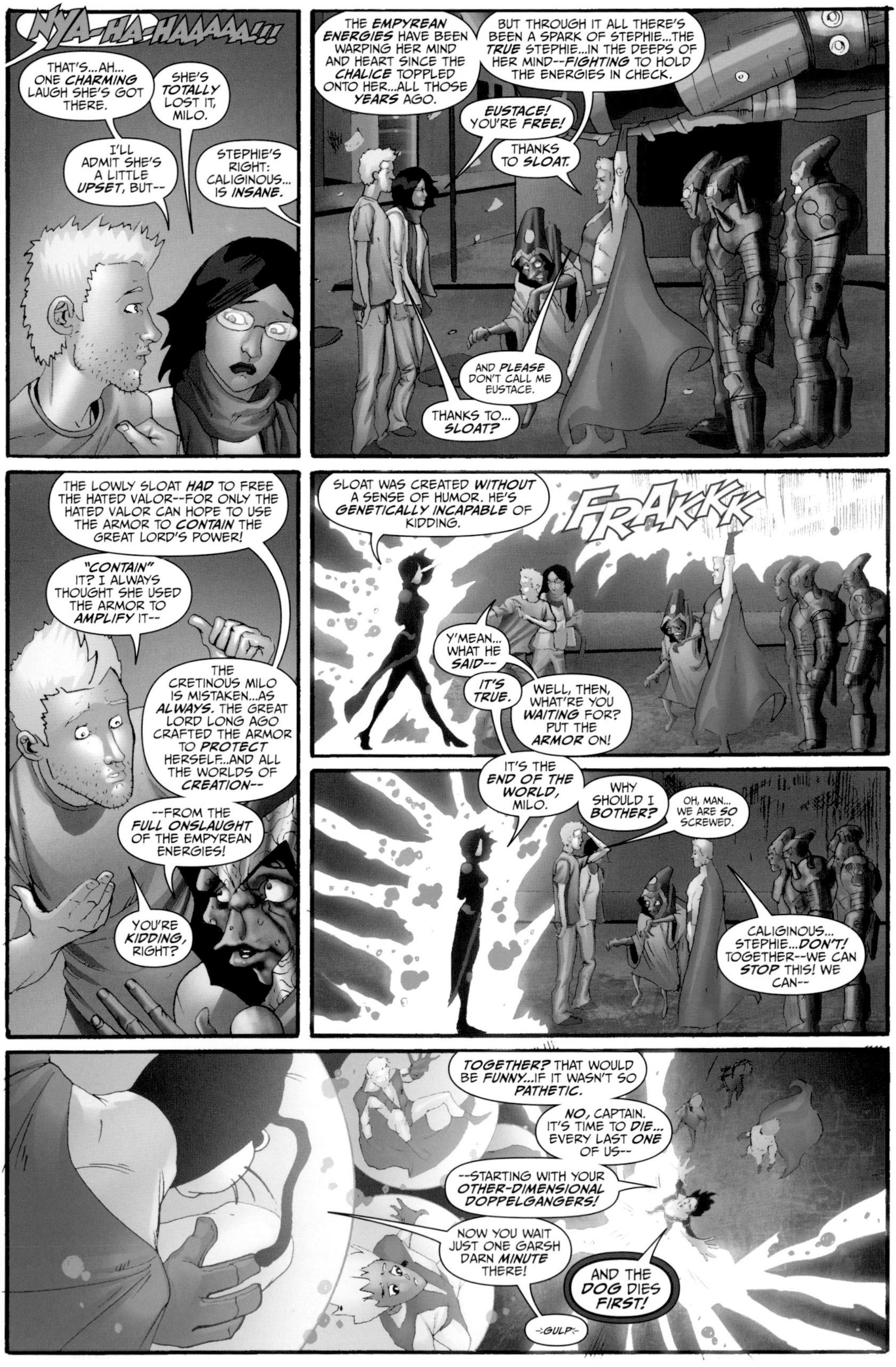
NYA-HA-HAAAAA!!!
THAT'S...AH... ONE CHARMING LAUGH SHE'S GOT THERE.
SHE'S TOTALLY LOST IT, MILO.
I'LL ADMIT SHE'S A LITTLE UPSET, BUT--
STEPHIE'S RIGHT: CALIGINOUS... IS INSANE.
THE EMPYREAN ENERGIES HAVE BEEN WARPING HER MIND AND HEART SINCE THE CHALICE TOPPLED ONTO HER...ALL THOSE YEARS AGO.
BUT THROUGH IT ALL THERE'S BEEN A SPARK OF STEPHIE...THE TRUE STEPHIE...IN THE DEEPS OF HER MIND--FIGHTING TO HOLD THE ENERGIES IN CHECK.
EUSTACE! YOU'RE FREE!
THANKS TO SLOAT.
AND PLEASE DON'T CALL ME EUSTACE.
THANKS TO... SLOAT?
THE LOWLY SLOAT HAD TO FREE THE HATED VALOR--FOR ONLY THE HATED VALOR CAN HOPE TO USE THE ARMOR TO CONTAIN THE GREAT LORD'S POWER!
"CONTAIN" IT? I ALWAYS THOUGHT SHE USED THE ARMOR TO AMPLIFY IT--
THE CRETINOUS MILO IS MISTAKEN...AS ALWAYS. THE GREAT LORD LONG AGO CRAFTED THE ARMOR TO PROTECT HERSELF...AND ALL THE WORLDS OF CREATION--
--FROM THE FULL ONSLAUGHT OF THE EMPYREAN ENERGIES!
YOU'RE KIDDING, RIGHT?
SLOAT WAS CREATED WITHOUT A SENSE OF HUMOR. HE'S GENETICALLY INCAPABLE OF KIDDING.
FRAKKK
Y'MEAN... WHAT HE SAID--
IT'S TRUE.
WELL, THEN, WHAT'RE YOU WAITING FOR? PUT THE ARMOR ON!
IT'S THE END OF THE WORLD, MILO.
WHY SHOULD I BOTHER?
OH, MAN... WE ARE SO SCREWED.
CALIGINOUS... STEPHIE...DON'T! TOGETHER--WE CAN STOP THIS! WE CAN--
TOGETHER? THAT WOULD BE FUNNY...IF IT WASN'T SO PATHETIC.
NO, CAPTAIN. IT'S TIME TO DIE... EVERY LAST ONE OF US--
--STARTING WITH YOUR OTHER-DIMENSIONAL DOPPELGANGERS!
NOW YOU WAIT JUST ONE GARSH DARN MINUTE THERE!
AND THE DOG DIES FIRST!
GULP

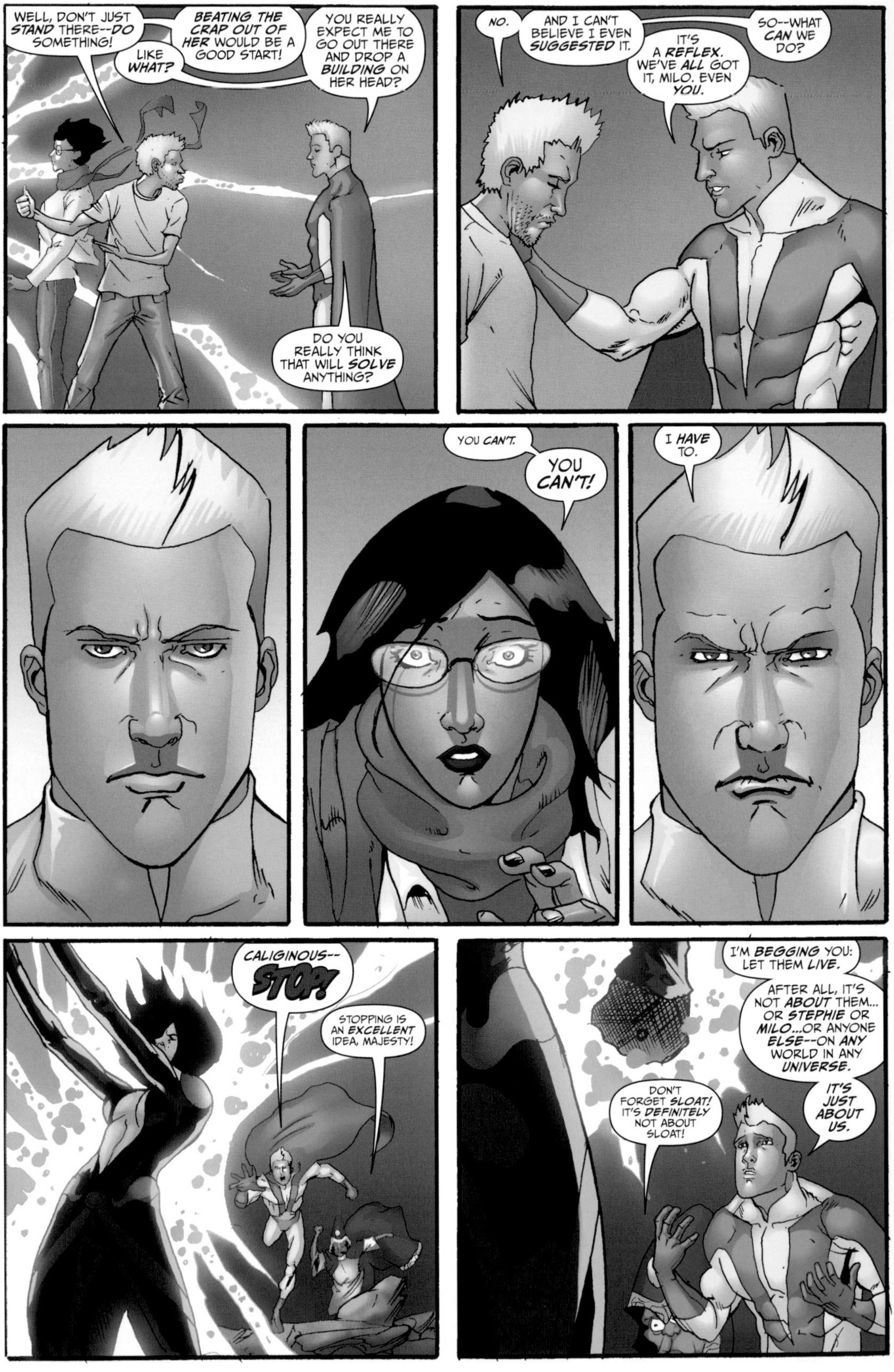
WELL, DON'T JUST STAND THERE--DO SOMETHING!
LIKE WHAT?
BEATING THE CRAP OUT OF HER WOULD BE A GOOD START!
YOU REALLY EXPECT ME TO GO OUT THERE AND DROP A BUILDING ON HER HEAD?
DO YOU REALLY THINK THAT WILL SOLVE ANYTHING?
NO.
AND I CAN'T BELIEVE I EVEN SUGGESTED IT.
IT'S A REFLEX. WE'VE ALL GOT IT, MILO. EVEN YOU.
SO--WHAT CAN WE DO?
YOU CAN'T.
YOU CAN'T!
I HAVE TO.
CALIGINOUS--
STOP!
STOPPING IS AN EXCELLENT IDEA, MAJESTY!
I'M BEGGING YOU: LET THEM LIVE.
AFTER ALL, IT'S NOT ABOUT THEM... OR STEPHIE OR MILO...OR ANYONE ELSE--ON ANY WORLD IN ANY UNIVERSE.
DON'T FORGET SLOAT! IT'S DEFINITELY NOT ABOUT SLOAT!
IT'S JUST ABOUT US.

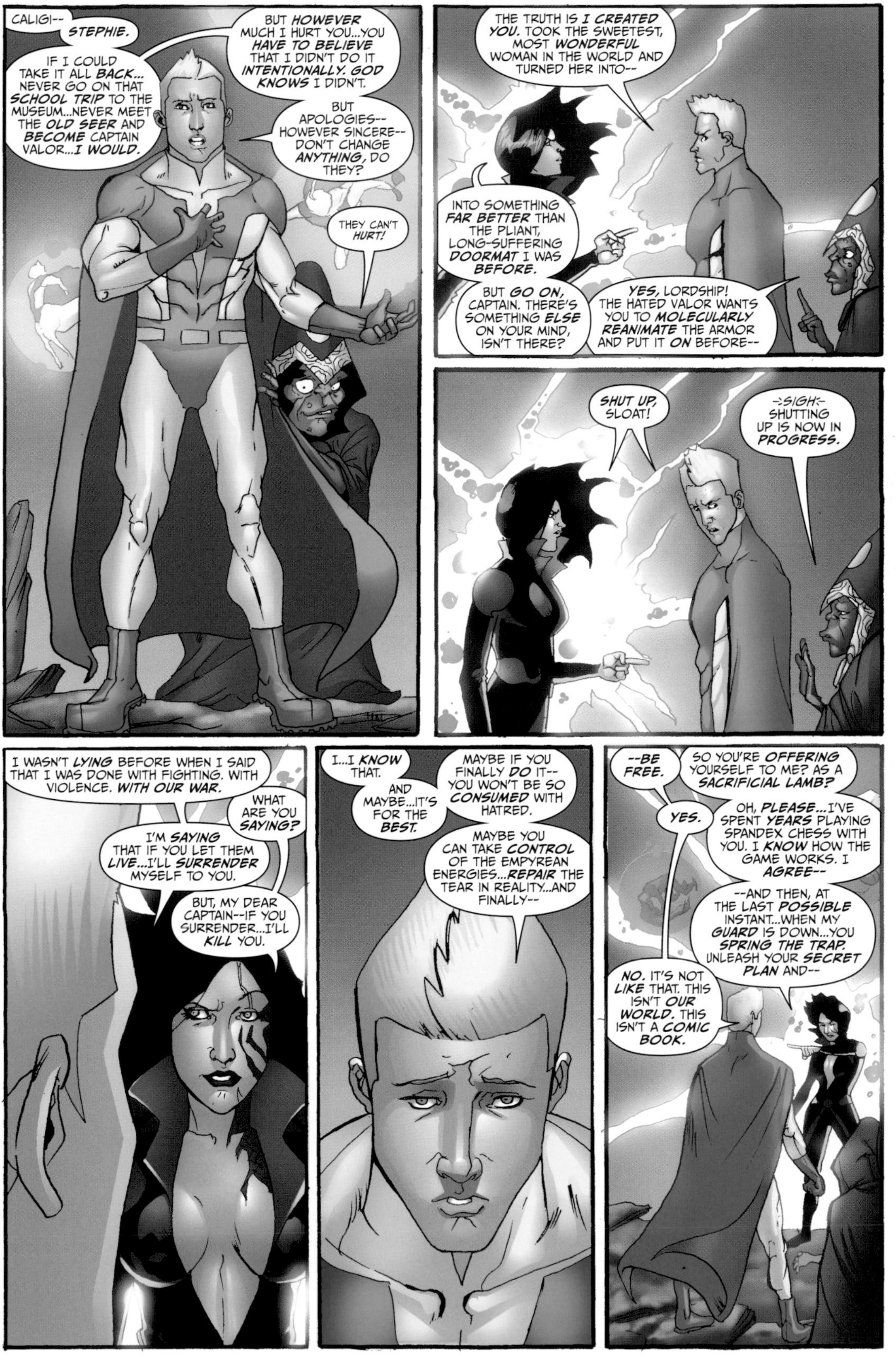
CALIGI--
STEPHIE.
IF I COULD TAKE IT ALL BACK... NEVER GO ON THAT SCHOOL TRIP TO THE MUSEUM...NEVER MEET THE OLD SEER AND BECOME CAPTAIN VALOR...I WOULD.
BUT HOWEVER MUCH I HURT YOU...YOU HAVE TO BELIEVE THAT I DIDN'T DO IT INTENTIONALLY. GOD KNOWS I DIDN'T.
BUT APOLOGIES--HOWEVER SINCERE--DON'T CHANGE ANYTHING, DO THEY?
THEY CAN'T HURT!
THE TRUTH IS I CREATED YOU. TOOK THE SWEETEST, MOST WONDERFUL WOMAN IN THE WORLD AND TURNED HER INTO--
INTO SOMETHING FAR BETTER THAN THE PLIANT, LONG-SUFFERING DOORMAT I WAS BEFORE.
BUT GO ON, CAPTAIN. THERE'S SOMETHING ELSE ON YOUR MIND, ISN'T THERE?
YES, LORDSHIP! THE HATED VALOR WANTS YOU TO MOLECULARLY REANIMATE THE ARMOR AND PUT IT ON BEFORE--
SHUT UP, SLOAT!
-SIGH- SHUTTING UP IS NOW IN PROGRESS.
I WASN'T LYING BEFORE WHEN I SAID THAT I WAS DONE WITH FIGHTING. WITH VIOLENCE. WITH OUR WAR.
WHAT ARE YOU SAYING?
I'M SAYING THAT IF YOU LET THEM LIVE...I'LL SURRENDER MYSELF TO YOU.
BUT, MY DEAR CAPTAIN--IF YOU SURRENDER...I'LL KILL YOU.
I...I KNOW THAT.
AND MAYBE...IT'S FOR THE BEST.
MAYBE IF YOU FINALLY DO IT--YOU WON'T BE SO CONSUMED WITH HATRED.
MAYBE YOU CAN TAKE CONTROL OF THE EMPYREAN ENERGIES...REPAIR THE TEAR IN REALITY...AND FINALLY--
--BE FREE.
SO YOU'RE OFFERING YOURSELF TO ME? AS A SACRIFICIAL LAMB?
YES.
OH, PLEASE...I'VE SPENT YEARS PLAYING SPANDEX CHESS WITH YOU. I KNOW HOW THE GAME WORKS. I AGREE--
--AND THEN, AT THE LAST POSSIBLE INSTANT...WHEN MY GUARD IS DOWN...YOU SPRING THE TRAP. UNLEASH YOUR SECRET PLAN AND--
NO. IT'S NOT LIKE THAT. THIS ISN'T OUR WORLD. THIS ISN'T A COMIC BOOK.

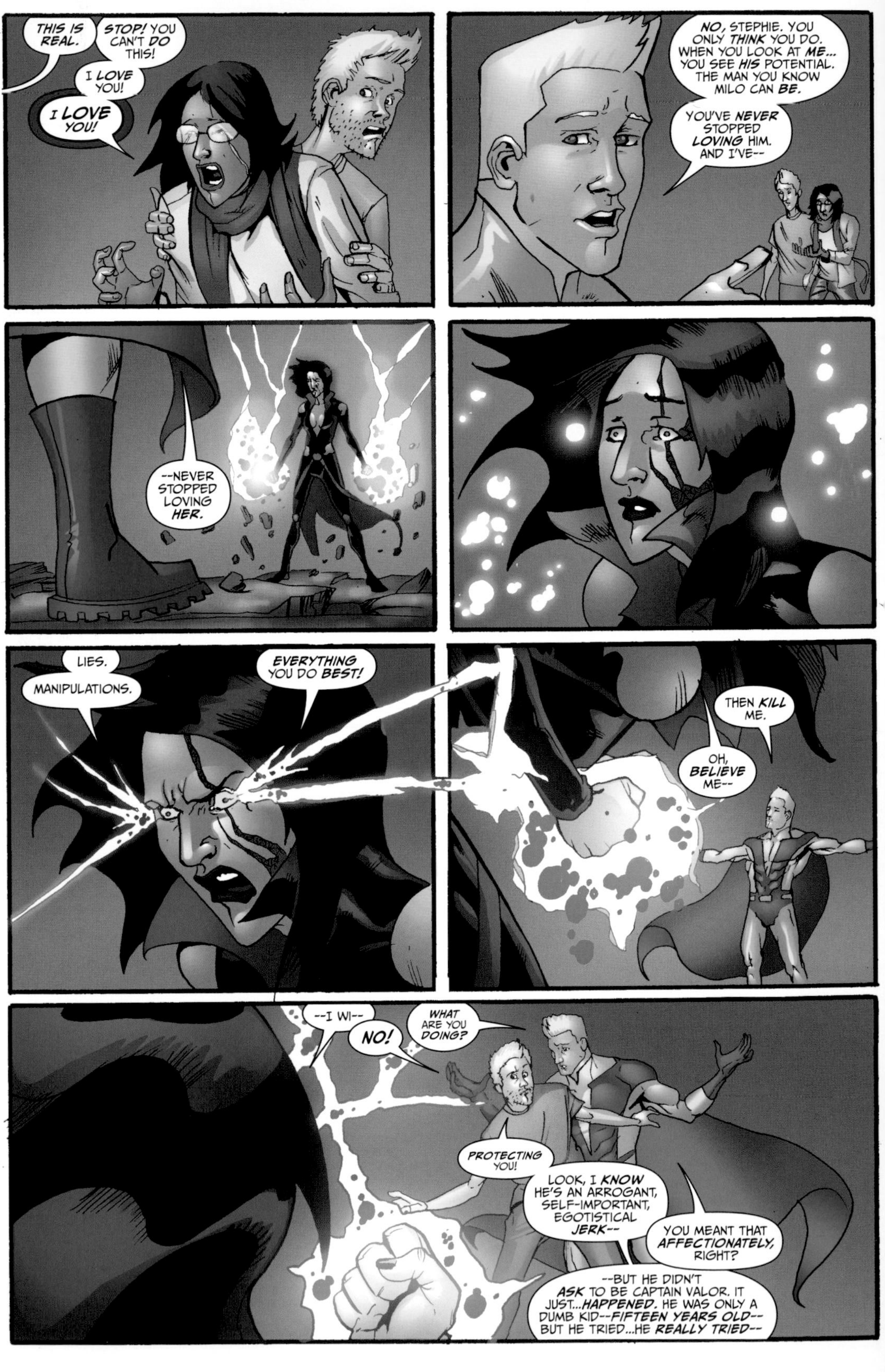
THIS IS REAL.
STOP! YOU CAN'T DO THIS!
I LOVE YOU!
I LOVE YOU!
NO, STEPHIE. YOU ONLY THINK YOU DO. WHEN YOU LOOK AT ME... YOU SEE HIS POTENTIAL. THE MAN YOU KNOW MILO CAN BE.
YOU'VE NEVER STOPPED LOVING HIM. AND I'VE--
--NEVER STOPPED LOVING HER.
LIES.
MANIPULATIONS.
EVERYTHING YOU DO BEST!
THEN KILL ME.
OH, BELIEVE ME--
--I WI--
NO!
WHAT ARE YOU DOING?
PROTECTING YOU!
LOOK, I KNOW HE'S AN ARROGANT, SELF-IMPORTANT, EGOTISTICAL JERK--
YOU MEANT THAT AFFECTIONATELY, RIGHT?
--BUT HE DIDN'T ASK TO BE CAPTAIN VALOR. IT JUST...HAPPENED. HE WAS ONLY A DUMB KID--FIFTEEN YEARS OLD--BUT HE TRIED...HE REALLY TRIED--

--T'DO THE *RIGHT* THING.

OKAY, SO HE SCREWED UP, *SPECTACULARLY.* BUT HE ALSO DID A LOT OF *GOOD* FOR YOUR WORLD, TOO.

I MEAN, WE *ALL* SCREW UP EVERY DAY, RIGHT? DO *HUGELY* STUPID THINGS THAT WE REGRET. *I SURE HAVE*--AND SO HAVE *YOU.*

BUT THAT DOESN'T MAKE *YOU* A VILLAIN.

AND IT DOESN'T MAKE *HIM* ONE, EITHER. *PLEASE*--

--LET HIM LIVE.

MILO--

--THANK YOU.

FLIK

POKT!

HEY!

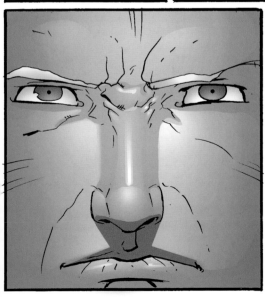

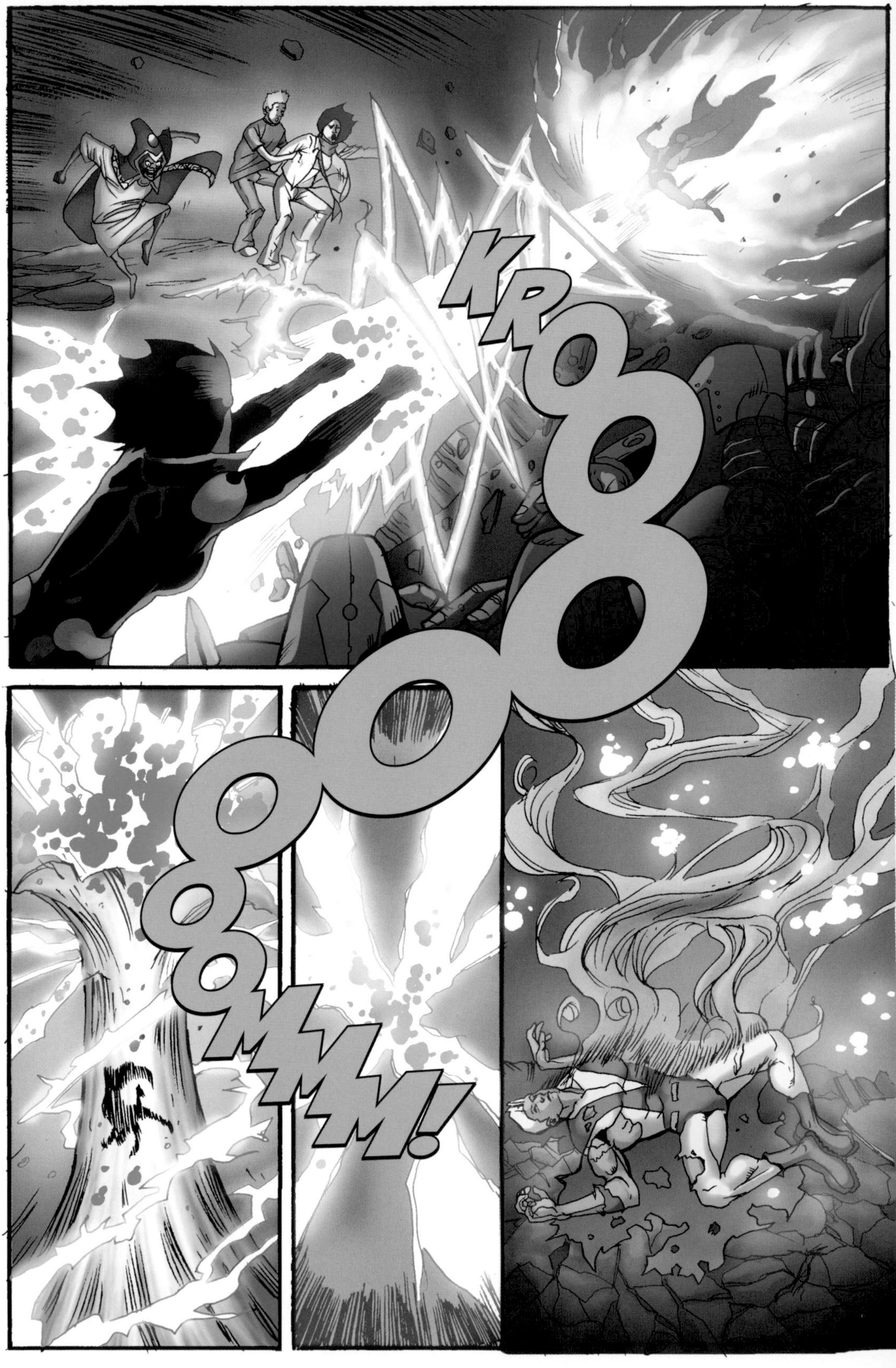
KRO8800000MMM!

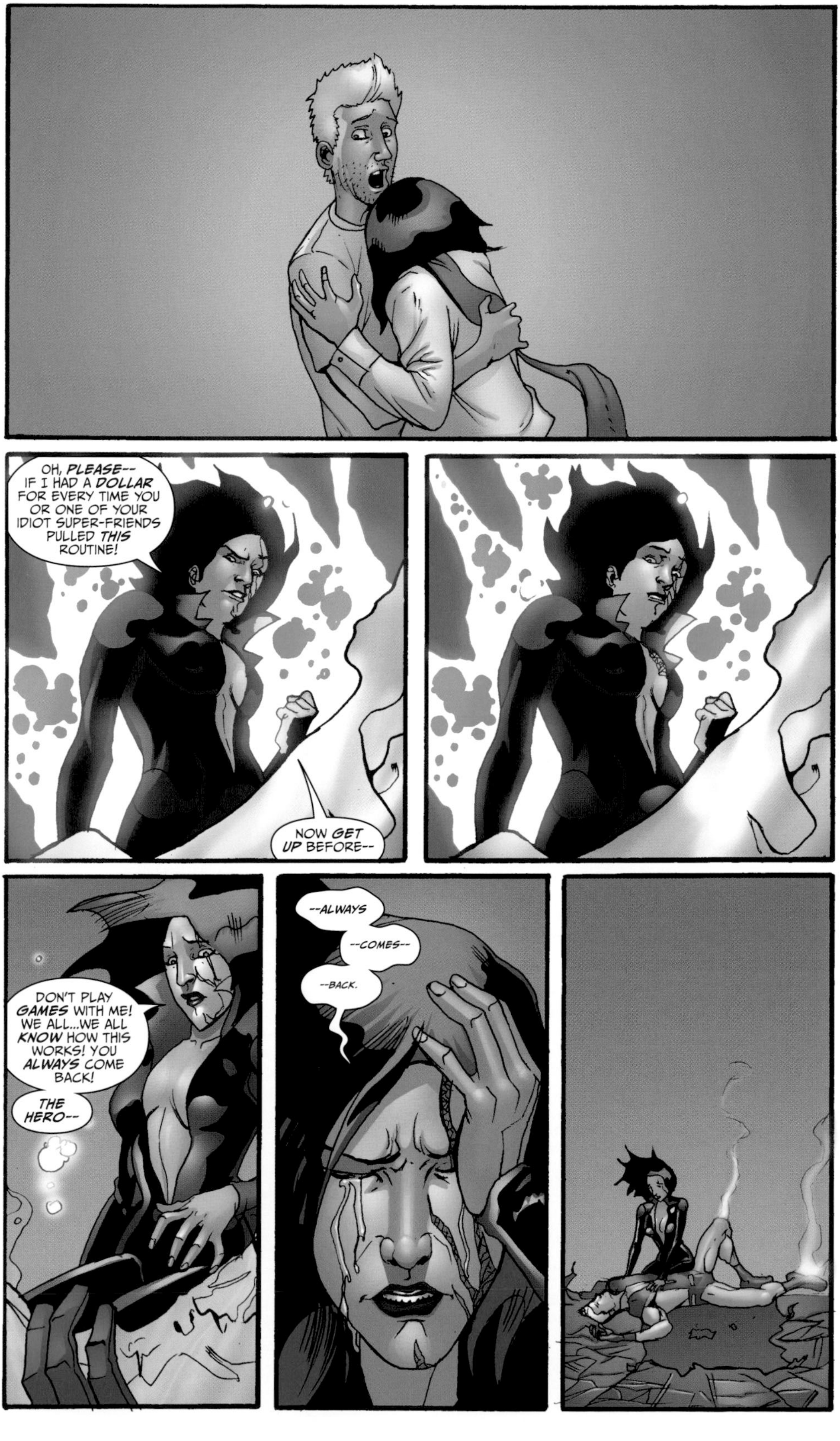
OH, *PLEASE*-- IF I HAD A *DOLLAR* FOR EVERY TIME YOU OR ONE OF YOUR IDIOT SUPER-FRIENDS PULLED *THIS* ROUTINE!
NOW *GET UP* BEFORE--
DON'T PLAY *GAMES* WITH ME! WE ALL...WE ALL *KNOW* HOW THIS WORKS! YOU *ALWAYS* COME BACK!
THE HERO--
--ALWAYS
--COMES--
--BACK.

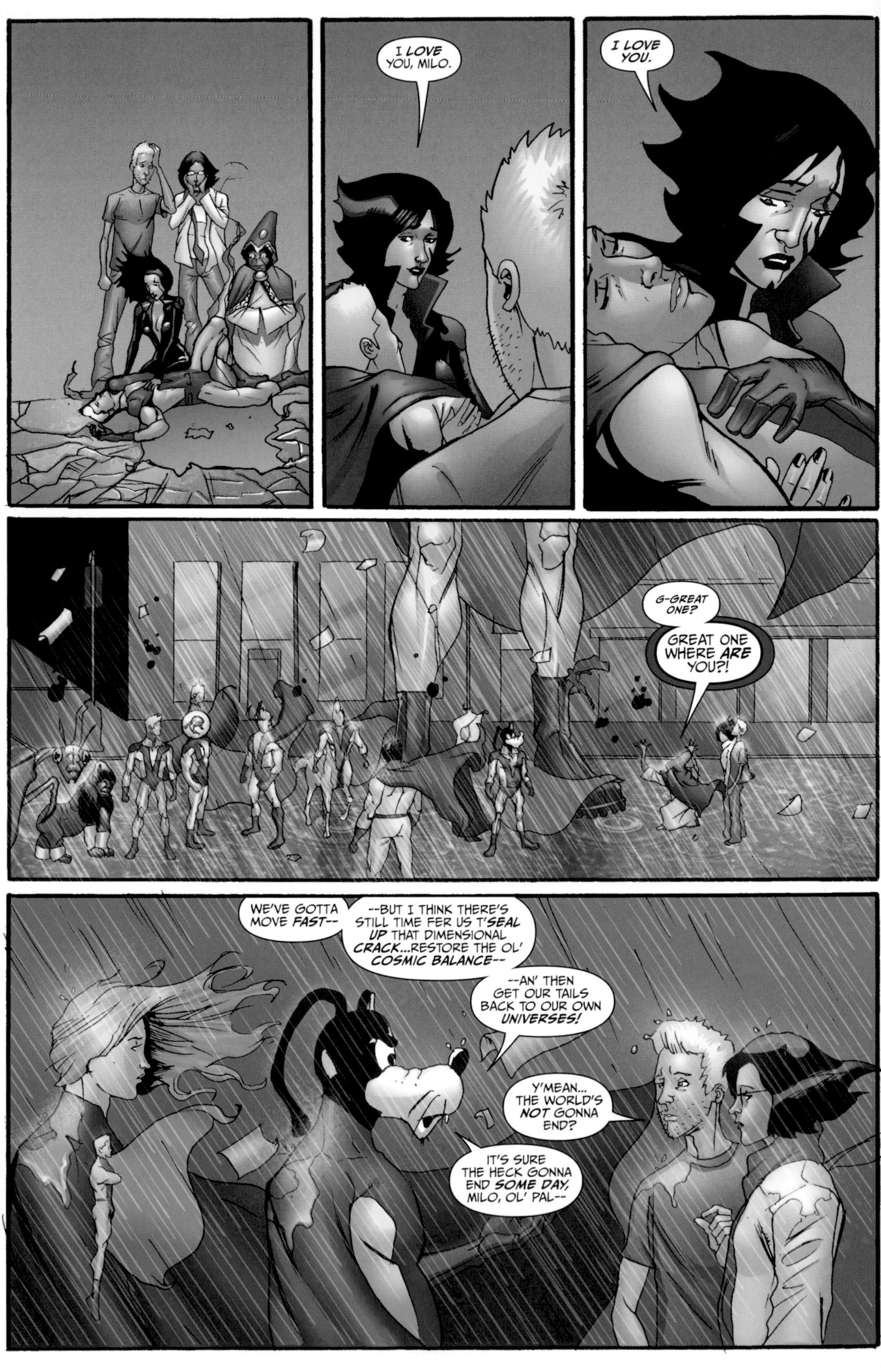
I LOVE YOU, MILO.
I LOVE YOU.
G-GREAT ONE?
GREAT ONE WHERE ARE YOU?!
WE'VE GOTTA MOVE FAST--
--BUT I THINK THERE'S STILL TIME FER US T'SEAL UP THAT DIMENSIONAL CRACK...RESTORE THE OL' COSMIC BALANCE--
--AN' THEN GET OUR TAILS BACK TO OUR OWN UNIVERSES!
Y'MEAN... THE WORLD'S NOT GONNA END?
IT'S SURE THE HECK GONNA END SOME DAY, MILO, OL' PAL--

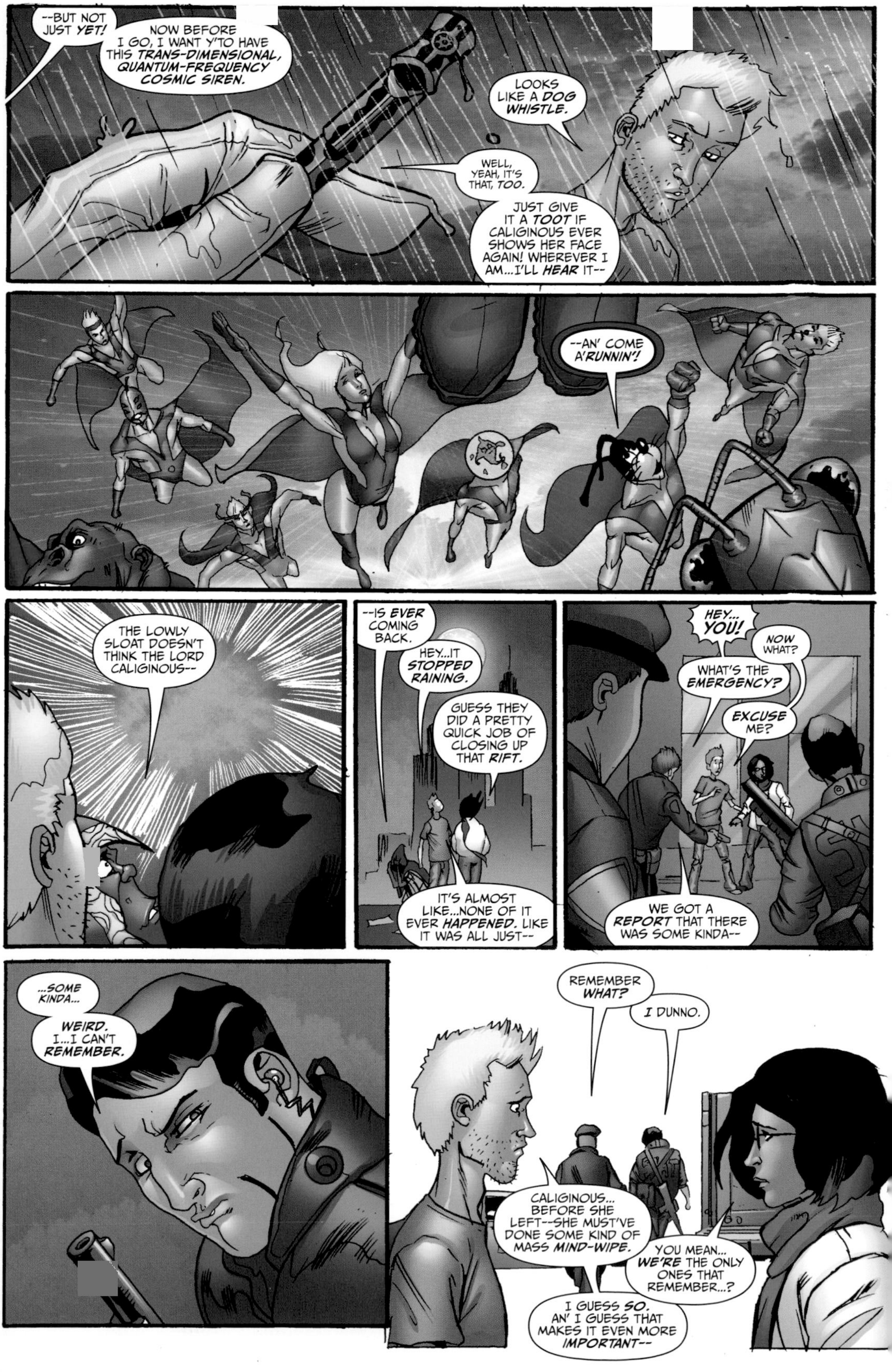
--BUT NOT JUST YET!
NOW BEFORE I GO, I WANT Y'TO HAVE THIS TRANS-DIMENSIONAL, QUANTUM-FREQUENCY COSMIC SIREN.
LOOKS LIKE A DOG WHISTLE.
WELL, YEAH, IT'S THAT, TOO.
JUST GIVE IT A TOOT IF CALIGINOUS EVER SHOWS HER FACE AGAIN! WHEREVER I AM...I'LL HEAR IT--
--AN' COME A'RUNNIN'!
THE LOWLY SLOAT DOESN'T THINK THE LORD CALIGINOUS--
--IS EVER COMING BACK.
HEY...IT STOPPED RAINING.
GUESS THEY DID A PRETTY QUICK JOB OF CLOSING UP THAT RIFT.
IT'S ALMOST LIKE...NONE OF IT EVER HAPPENED. LIKE IT WAS ALL JUST--
HEY... YOU!
NOW WHAT?
WHAT'S THE EMERGENCY?
EXCUSE ME?
WE GOT A REPORT THAT THERE WAS SOME KINDA--
...SOME KINDA...
WEIRD. I...I CAN'T REMEMBER.
REMEMBER WHAT?
I DUNNO.
CALIGINOUS... BEFORE SHE LEFT--SHE MUST'VE DONE SOME KIND OF MASS MIND-WIPE.
YOU MEAN... WE'RE THE ONLY ONES THAT REMEMBER...?
I GUESS SO. AN' I GUESS THAT MAKES IT EVEN MORE IMPORTANT--

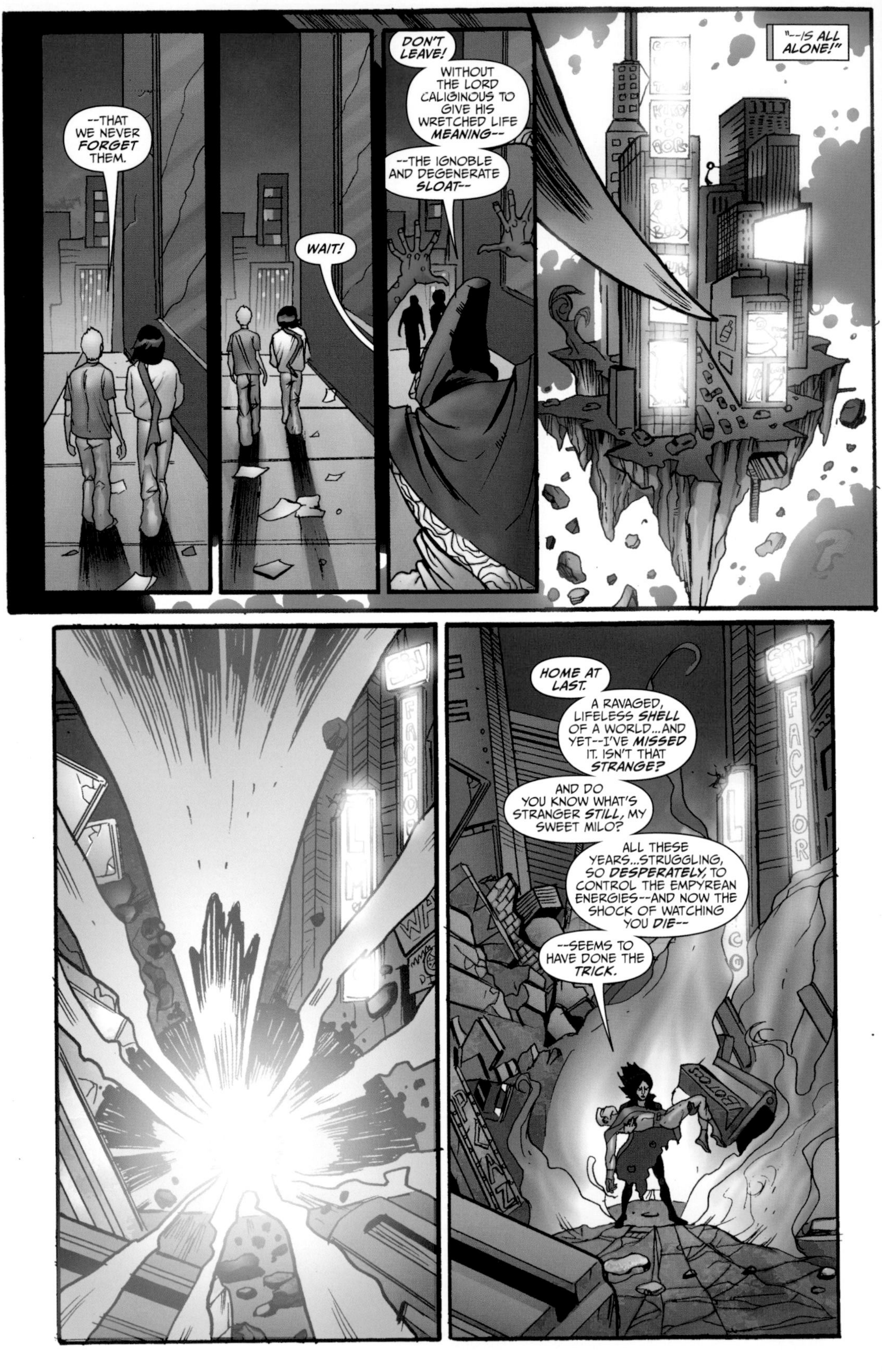

--THAT WE NEVER FORGET THEM.
WAIT!
DON'T LEAVE!
WITHOUT THE LORD CALIGINOUS TO GIVE HIS WRETCHED LIFE MEANING--
--THE IGNOBLE AND DEGENERATE SLOAT--
"--IS ALL ALONE!"
SIN
FACTOR
HOME AT LAST.
A RAVAGED, LIFELESS SHELL OF A WORLD...AND YET--I'VE MISSED IT. ISN'T THAT STRANGE?
AND DO YOU KNOW WHAT'S STRANGER STILL, MY SWEET MILO?
ALL THESE YEARS...STRUGGLING, SO DESPERATELY, TO CONTROL THE EMPYREAN ENERGIES--AND NOW THE SHOCK OF WATCHING YOU DIE--
--SEEMS TO HAVE DONE THE TRICK.

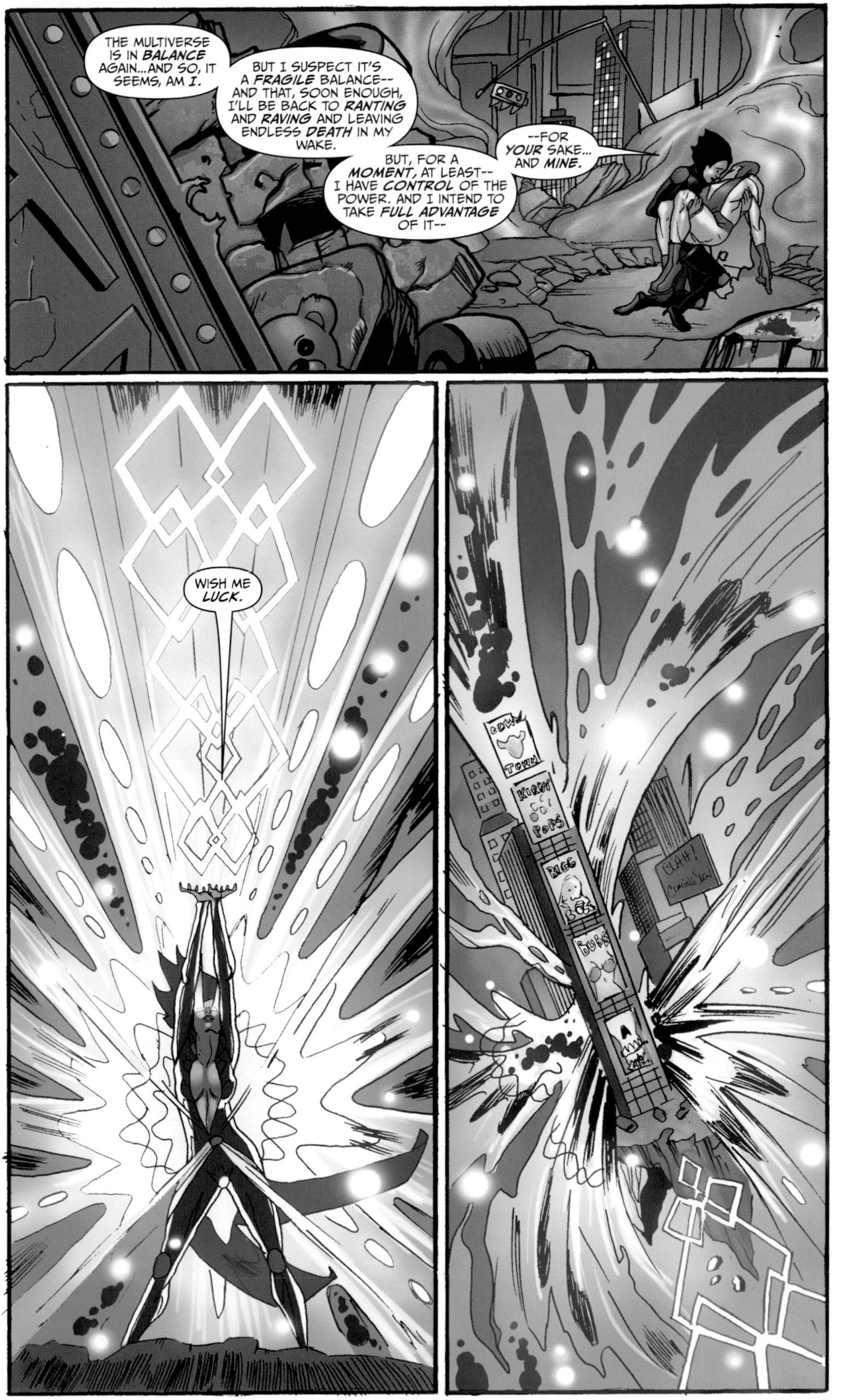
THE MULTIVERSE IS IN BALANCE AGAIN...AND SO, IT SEEMS, AM I.
BUT I SUSPECT IT'S A FRAGILE BALANCE--AND THAT, SOON ENOUGH, I'LL BE BACK TO RANTING AND RAVING AND LEAVING ENDLESS DEATH IN MY WAKE.
BUT, FOR A MOMENT, AT LEAST--I HAVE CONTROL OF THE POWER. AND I INTEND TO TAKE FULL ADVANTAGE OF IT--
--FOR YOUR SAKE... AND MINE.
WISH ME LUCK.

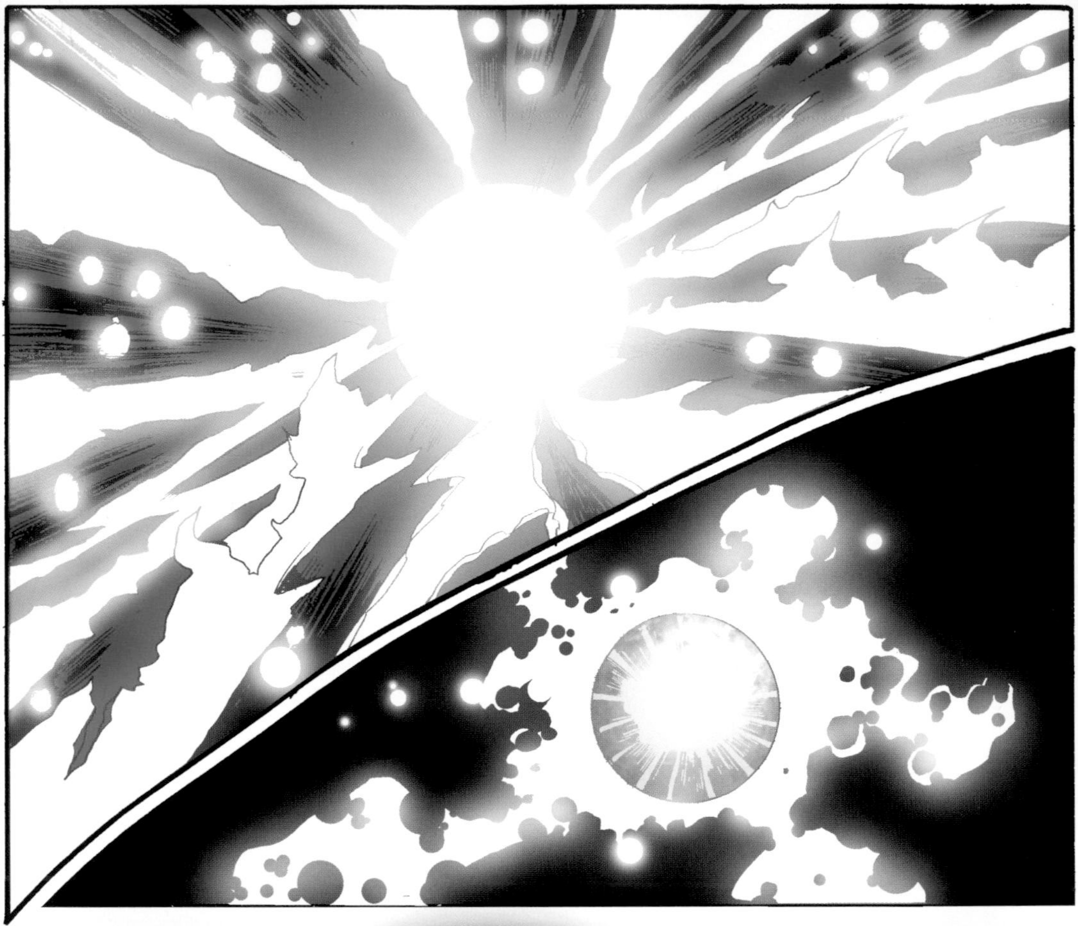

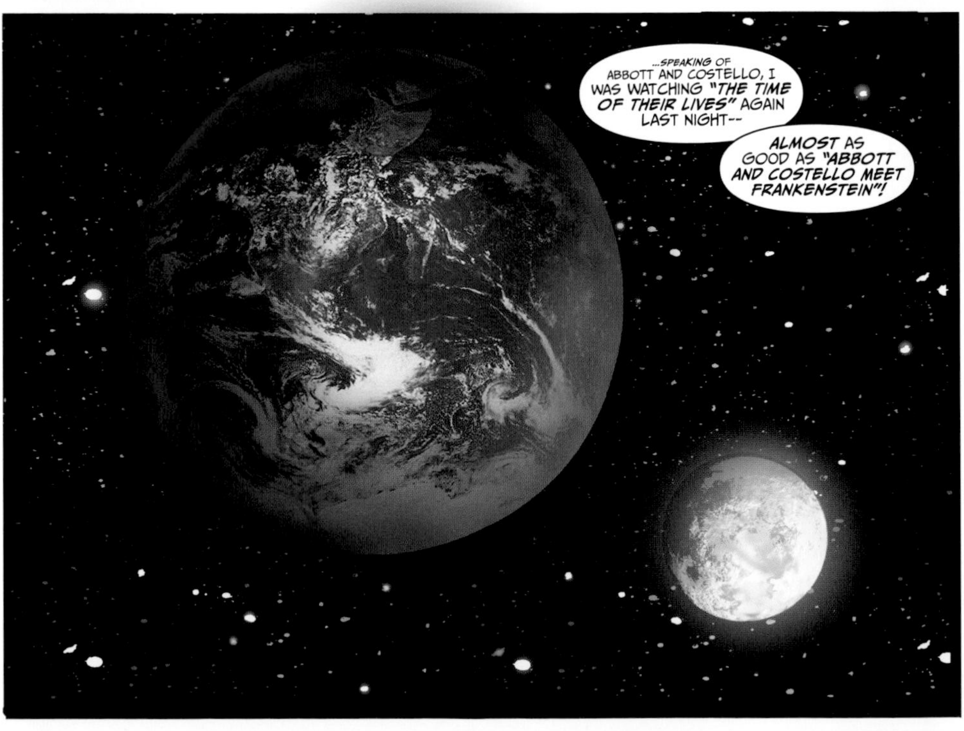
...SPEAKING OF ABBOTT AND COSTELLO, I WAS WATCHING "THE TIME OF THEIR LIVES" AGAIN LAST NIGHT--
ALMOST AS GOOD AS "ABBOTT AND COSTELLO MEET FRANKENSTEIN"!

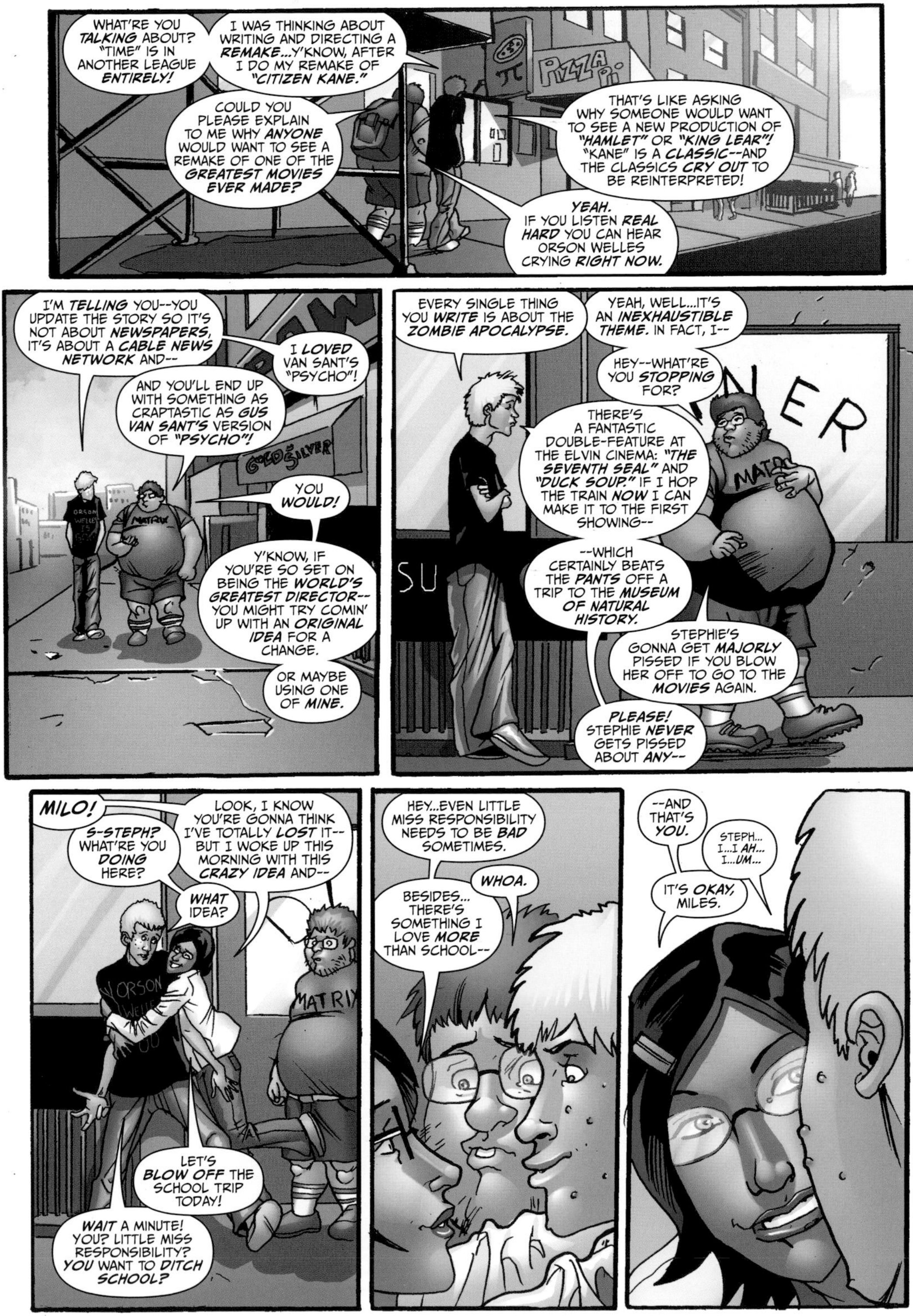
WHAT'RE YOU TALKING ABOUT? "TIME" IS IN ANOTHER LEAGUE ENTIRELY!
I WAS THINKING ABOUT WRITING AND DIRECTING A REMAKE...Y'KNOW, AFTER I DO MY REMAKE OF "CITIZEN KANE."
PIZZA PI
COULD YOU PLEASE EXPLAIN TO ME WHY ANYONE WOULD WANT TO SEE A REMAKE OF ONE OF THE GREATEST MOVIES EVER MADE?
THAT'S LIKE ASKING WHY SOMEONE WOULD WANT TO SEE A NEW PRODUCTION OF "HAMLET" OR "KING LEAR"! "KANE" IS A CLASSIC--AND THE CLASSICS CRY OUT TO BE REINTERPRETED!
YEAH. IF YOU LISTEN REAL HARD YOU CAN HEAR ORSON WELLES CRYING RIGHT NOW.
I'M TELLING YOU--YOU UPDATE THE STORY SO IT'S NOT ABOUT NEWSPAPERS, IT'S ABOUT A CABLE NEWS NETWORK AND--
I LOVED VAN SANT'S "PSYCHO"!
AND YOU'LL END UP WITH SOMETHING AS CRAPTASTIC AS GUS VAN SANT'S VERSION OF "PSYCHO"!
GOLD SILVER
ORSON WELLES IS GOD
MATRIX
YOU WOULD!
Y'KNOW, IF YOU'RE SO SET ON BEING THE WORLD'S GREATEST DIRECTOR--YOU MIGHT TRY COMIN' UP WITH AN ORIGINAL IDEA FOR A CHANGE.
OR MAYBE USING ONE OF MINE.
EVERY SINGLE THING YOU WRITE IS ABOUT THE ZOMBIE APOCALYPSE.
YEAH, WELL...IT'S AN INEXHAUSTIBLE THEME. IN FACT, I--
HEY--WHAT'RE YOU STOPPING FOR?
THERE'S A FANTASTIC DOUBLE-FEATURE AT THE ELVIN CINEMA: "THE SEVENTH SEAL" AND "DUCK SOUP." IF I HOP THE TRAIN NOW I CAN MAKE IT TO THE FIRST SHOWING--
--WHICH CERTAINLY BEATS THE PANTS OFF A TRIP TO THE MUSEUM OF NATURAL HISTORY.
STEPHIE'S GONNA GET MAJORLY PISSED IF YOU BLOW HER OFF TO GO TO THE MOVIES AGAIN.
PLEASE! STEPHIE NEVER GETS PISSED ABOUT ANY--
MILO!
S-STEPH? WHAT'RE YOU DOING HERE?
LOOK, I KNOW YOU'RE GONNA THINK I'VE TOTALLY LOST IT--BUT I WOKE UP THIS MORNING WITH THIS CRAZY IDEA AND--
WHAT IDEA?
ORSON WELLES
MATRIX
LET'S BLOW OFF THE SCHOOL TRIP TODAY!
WAIT A MINUTE! YOU? LITTLE MISS RESPONSIBILITY? YOU WANT TO DITCH SCHOOL?
HEY...EVEN LITTLE MISS RESPONSIBILITY NEEDS TO BE BAD SOMETIMES.
WHOA.
BESIDES... THERE'S SOMETHING I LOVE MORE THAN SCHOOL--
--AND THAT'S YOU.
STEPH... I...I AH... I...UM...
IT'S OKAY, MILES.

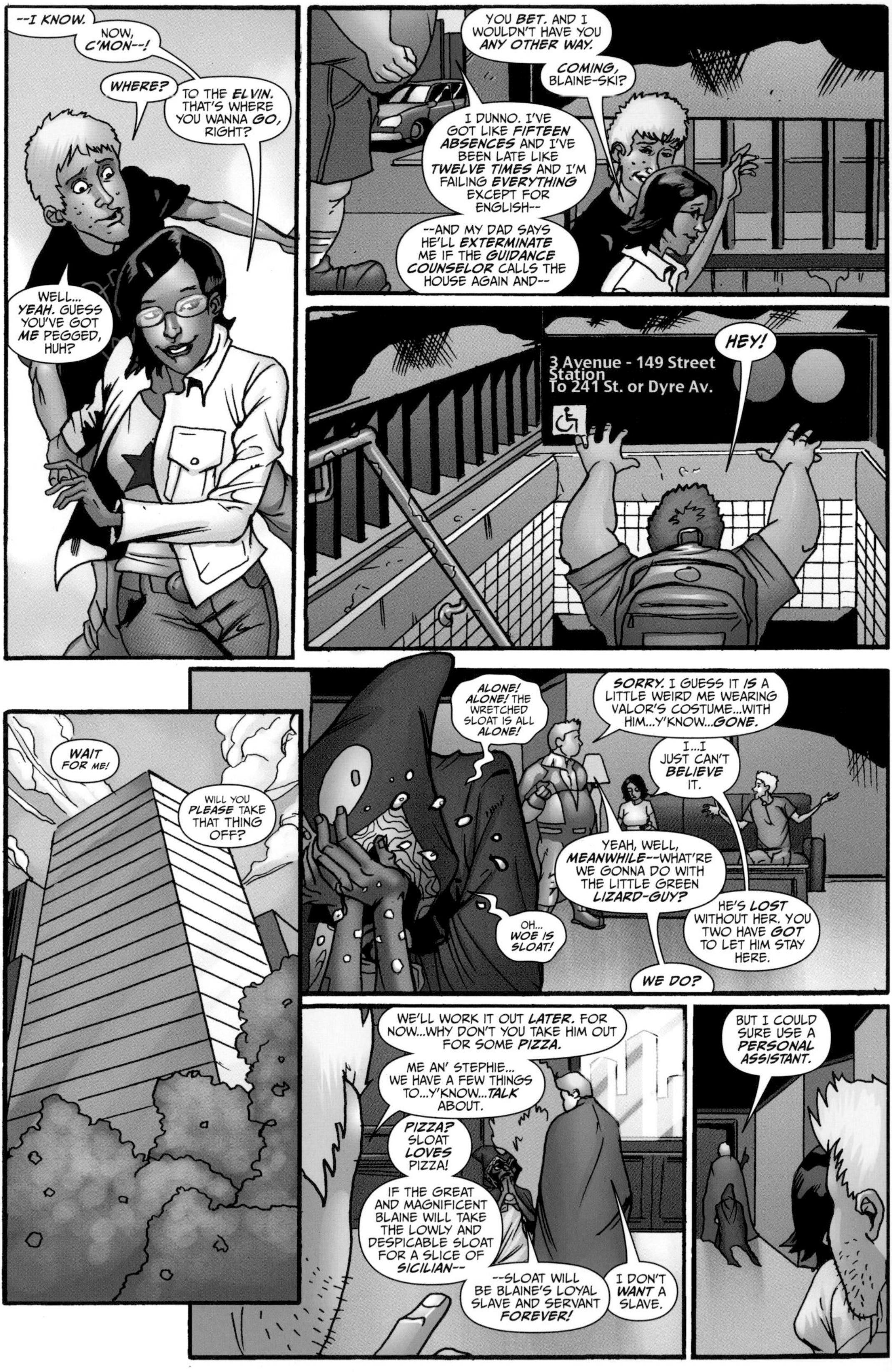
--I KNOW.
NOW, C'MON--!
WHERE?
TO THE ELVIN. THAT'S WHERE YOU WANNA GO, RIGHT?
WELL... YEAH. GUESS YOU'VE GOT ME PEGGED, HUH?
YOU BET. AND I WOULDN'T HAVE YOU ANY OTHER WAY.
COMING, BLAINE-SKI?
I DUNNO. I'VE GOT LIKE FIFTEEN ABSENCES AND I'VE BEEN LATE LIKE TWELVE TIMES AND I'M FAILING EVERYTHING EXCEPT FOR ENGLISH--
--AND MY DAD SAYS HE'LL EXTERMINATE ME IF THE GUIDANCE COUNSELOR CALLS THE HOUSE AGAIN AND--
3 Avenue - 149 Street Station
To 241 St. or Dyre Av.
HEY!
WAIT FOR ME!
WILL YOU PLEASE TAKE THAT THING OFF?
ALONE! ALONE! THE WRETCHED SLOAT IS ALL ALONE!
SORRY. I GUESS IT IS A LITTLE WEIRD ME WEARING VALOR'S COSTUME...WITH HIM...Y'KNOW...GONE.
I...I JUST CAN'T BELIEVE IT.
YEAH, WELL, MEANWHILE--WHAT'RE WE GONNA DO WITH THE LITTLE GREEN LIZARD-GUY?
OH... WOE IS SLOAT!
HE'S LOST WITHOUT HER. YOU TWO HAVE GOT TO LET HIM STAY HERE.
WE DO?
WE'LL WORK IT OUT LATER. FOR NOW...WHY DON'T YOU TAKE HIM OUT FOR SOME PIZZA.
ME AN' STEPHIE... WE HAVE A FEW THINGS TO...Y'KNOW...TALK ABOUT.
PIZZA? SLOAT LOVES PIZZA!
IF THE GREAT AND MAGNIFICENT BLAINE WILL TAKE THE LOWLY AND DESPICABLE SLOAT FOR A SLICE OF SICILIAN--
--SLOAT WILL BE BLAINE'S LOYAL SLAVE AND SERVANT FOREVER!
I DON'T WANT A SLAVE.
BUT I COULD SURE USE A PERSONAL ASSISTANT.

I JUST WANTED TO *SAY* THAT I...THAT IS...ALL THE *STUFF* I...I MEAN THE THING *IS*--

IT'S OKAY, MILES.

I KNOW.

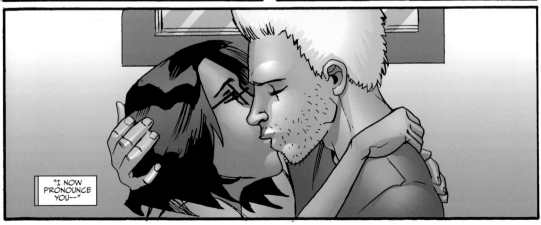

"I NOW PRONOUNCE YOU--"

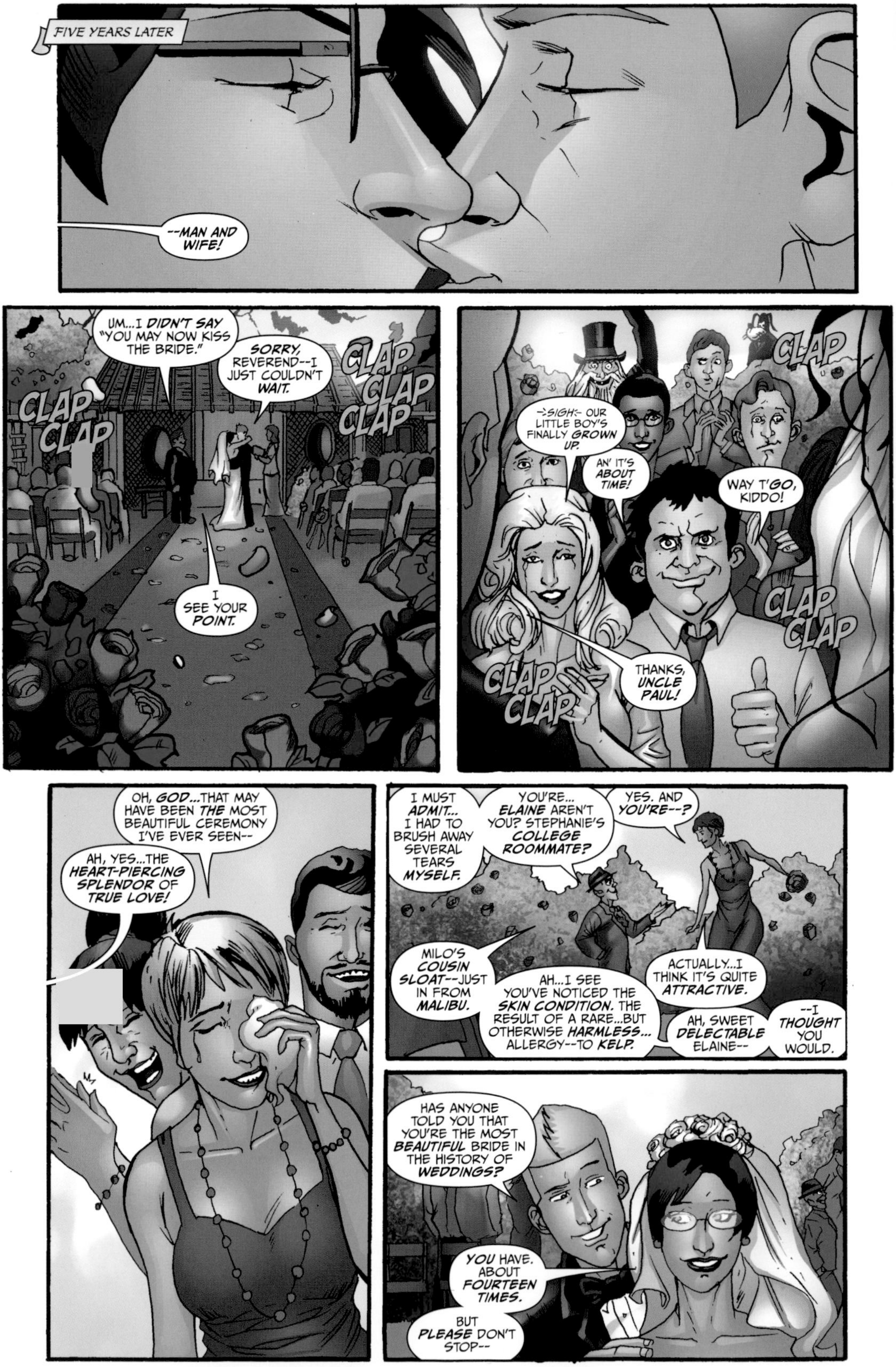
FIVE YEARS LATER
--MAN AND WIFE!
UM...I DIDN'T SAY "YOU MAY NOW KISS THE BRIDE."
SORRY, REVEREND--I JUST COULDN'T WAIT.
CLAP CLAP
CLAP CLAP CLAP
I SEE YOUR POINT.
CLAP
-SIGH- OUR LITTLE BOY'S FINALLY GROWN UP.
AN' IT'S ABOUT TIME!
WAY T'GO, KIDDO!
CLAP CLAP
CLAP CLAP
THANKS, UNCLE PAUL!
OH, GOD...THAT MAY HAVE BEEN THE MOST BEAUTIFUL CEREMONY I'VE EVER SEEN--
AH, YES...THE HEART-PIERCING SPLENDOR OF TRUE LOVE!
I MUST ADMIT... I HAD TO BRUSH AWAY SEVERAL TEARS MYSELF.
YOU'RE... ELAINE AREN'T YOU? STEPHANIE'S COLLEGE ROOMMATE?
YES. AND YOU'RE--?
MILO'S COUSIN SLOAT--JUST IN FROM MALIBU.
AH...I SEE YOU'VE NOTICED THE SKIN CONDITION. THE RESULT OF A RARE...BUT OTHERWISE HARMLESS... ALLERGY--TO KELP.
ACTUALLY...I THINK IT'S QUITE ATTRACTIVE.
AH, SWEET DELECTABLE ELAINE--
--I THOUGHT YOU WOULD.
HAS ANYONE TOLD YOU THAT YOU'RE THE MOST BEAUTIFUL BRIDE IN THE HISTORY OF WEDDINGS?
YOU HAVE. ABOUT FOURTEEN TIMES.
BUT PLEASE DON'T STOP--

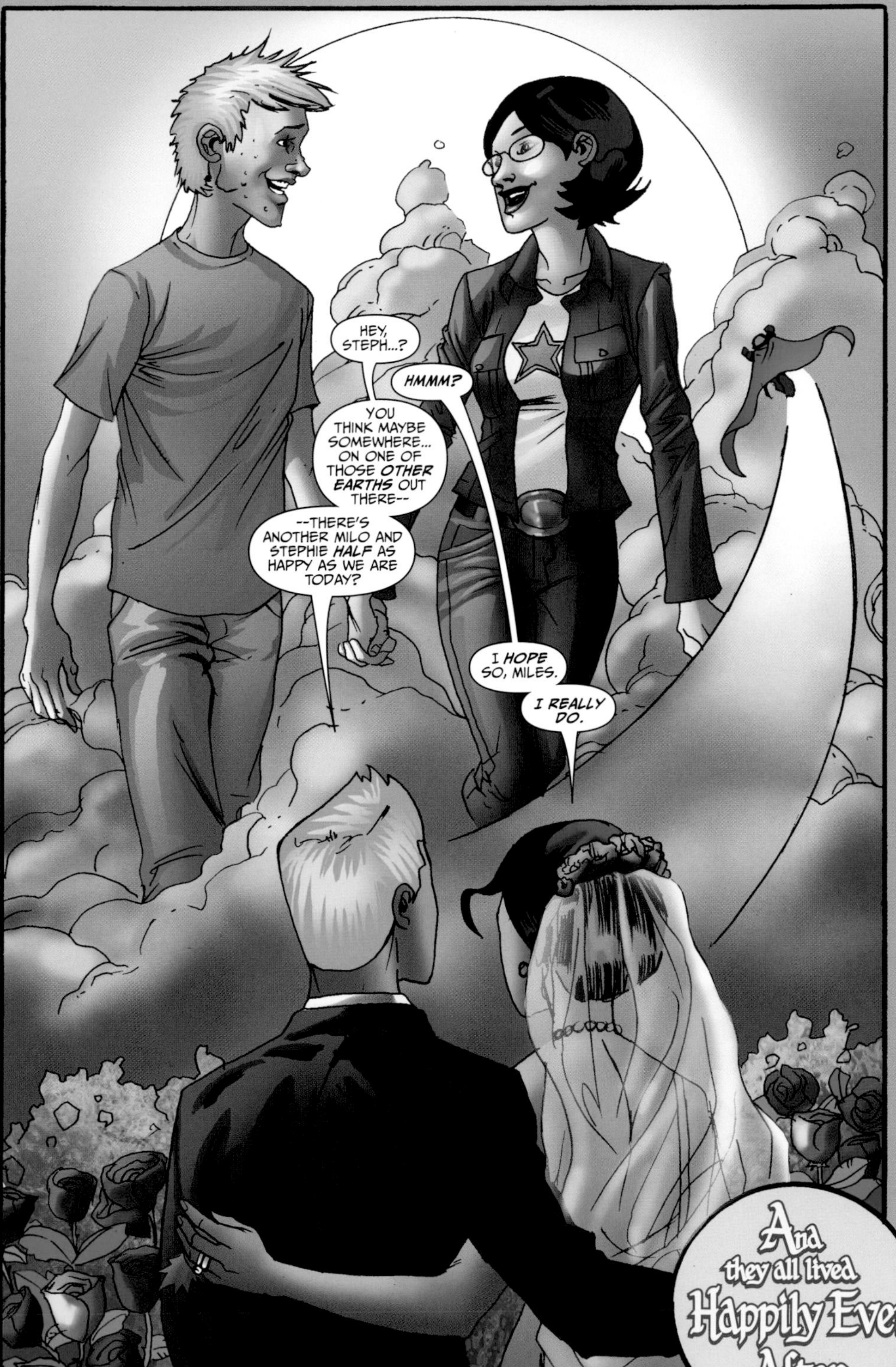
HEY, STEPH...?
HMMM?
YOU THINK MAYBE SOMEWHERE... ON ONE OF THOSE OTHER EARTHS OUT THERE--
--THERE'S ANOTHER MILO AND STEPHIE HALF AS HAPPY AS WE ARE TODAY?
I HOPE SO, MILES.
I REALLY DO.
And they all lived Happily Ever After

COVER GALLERY

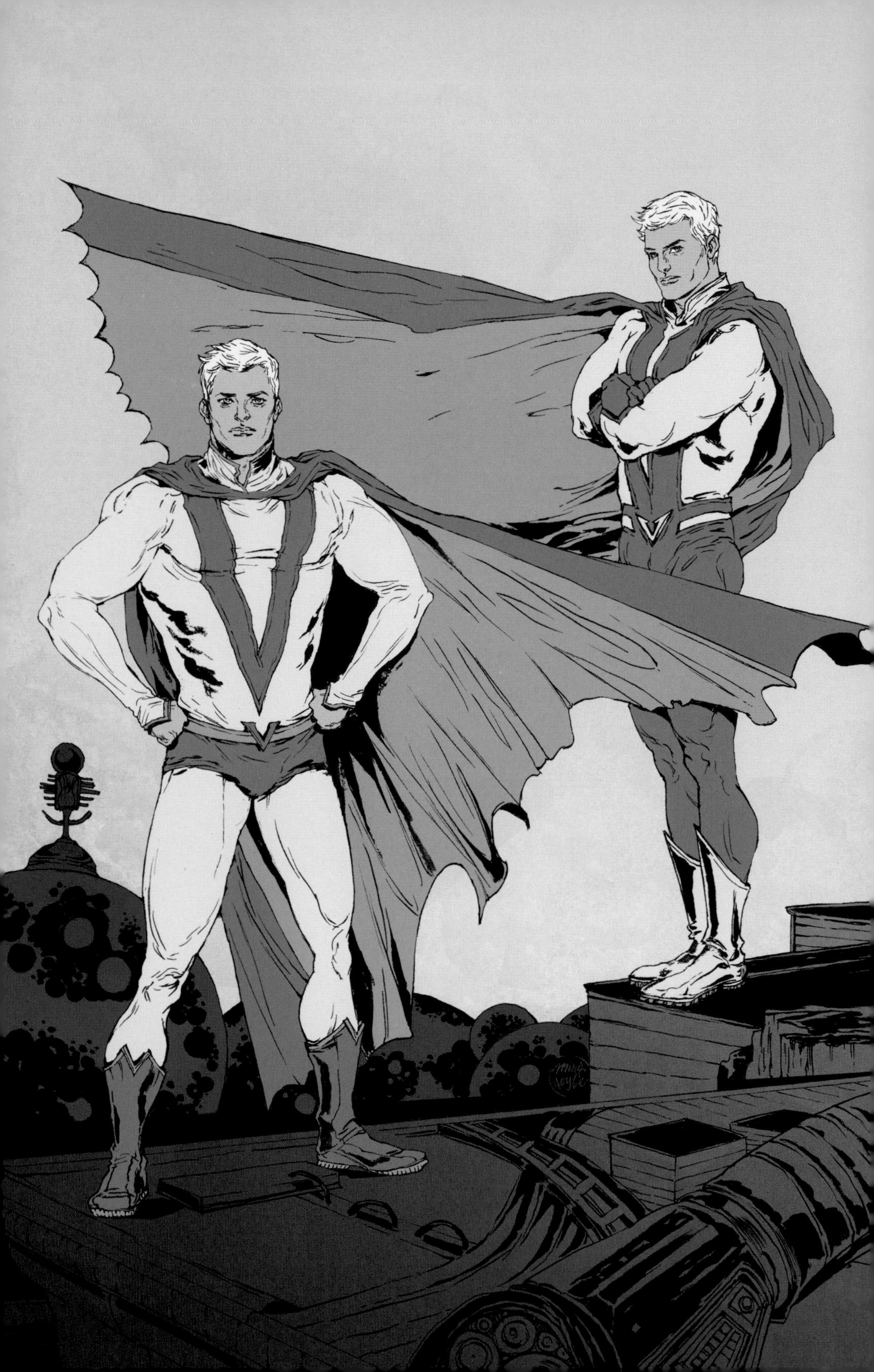

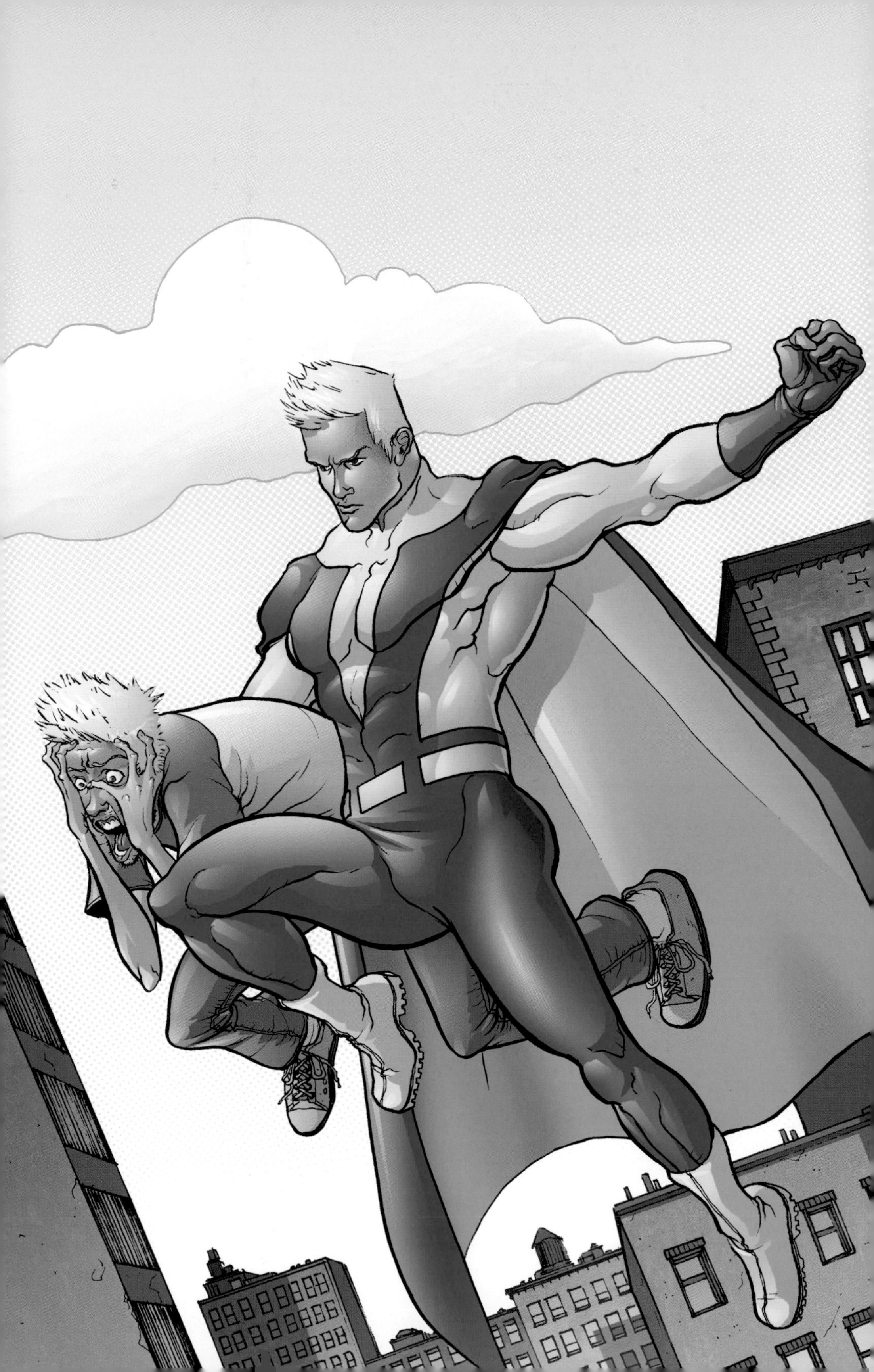

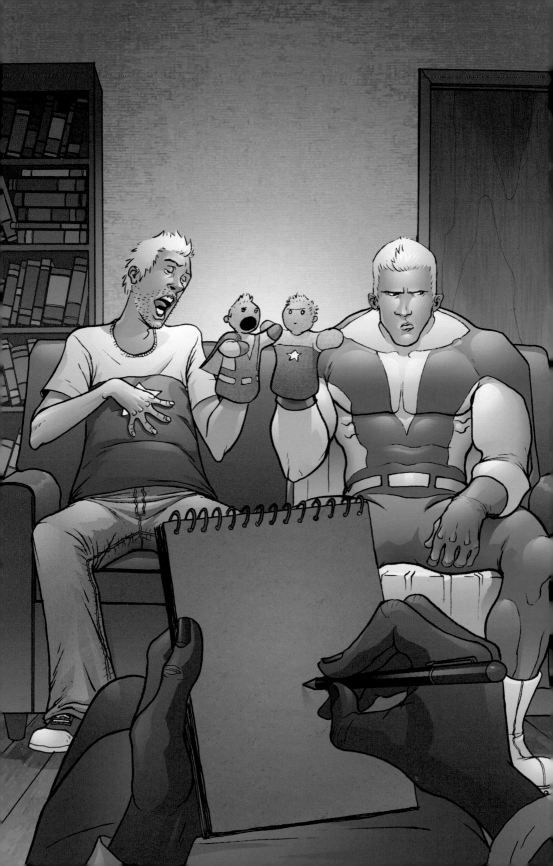

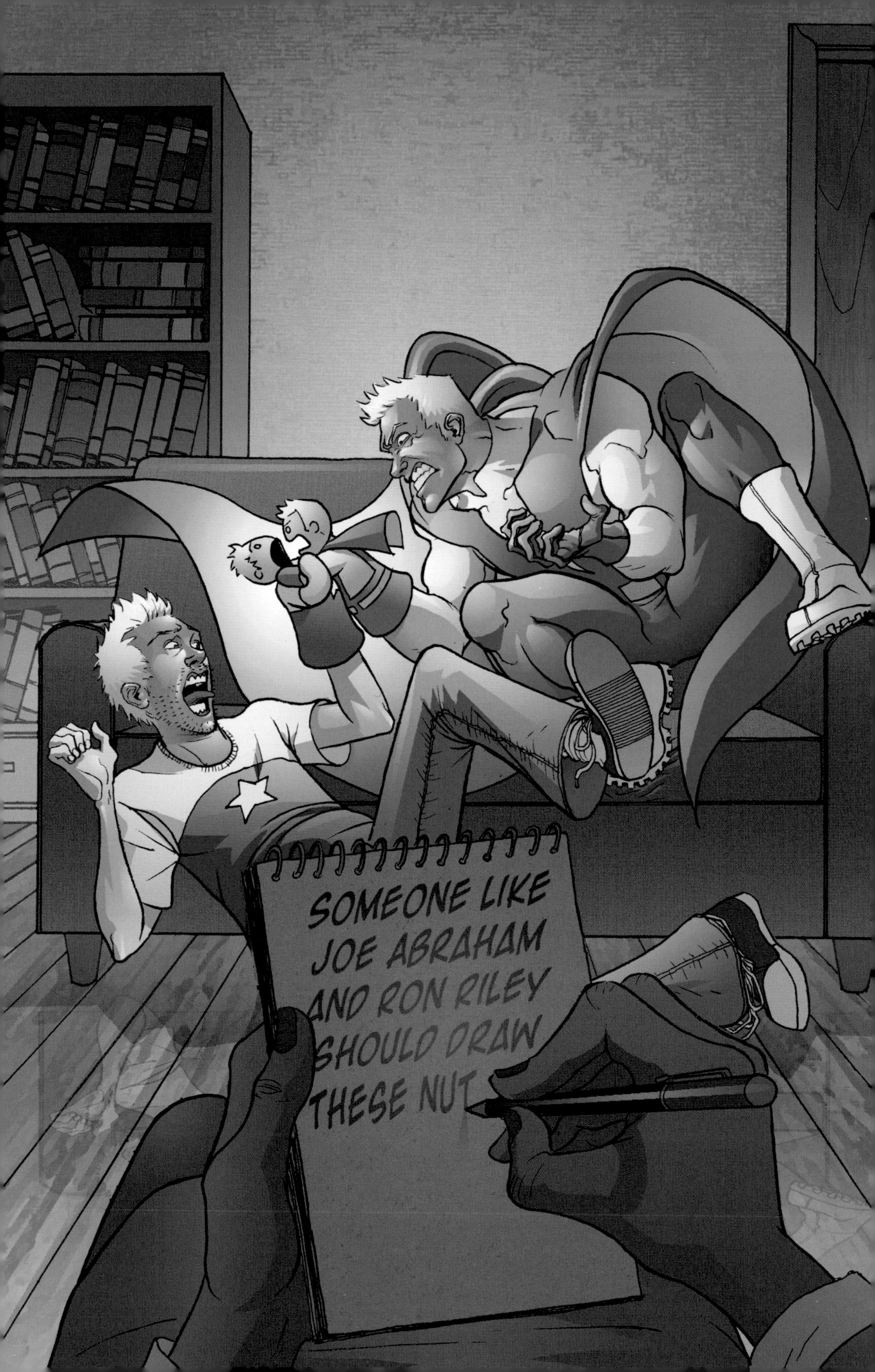
SOMEONE LIKE
JOE ABRAHAM
AND RON RILEY
SHOULD DRAW
THESE NUT

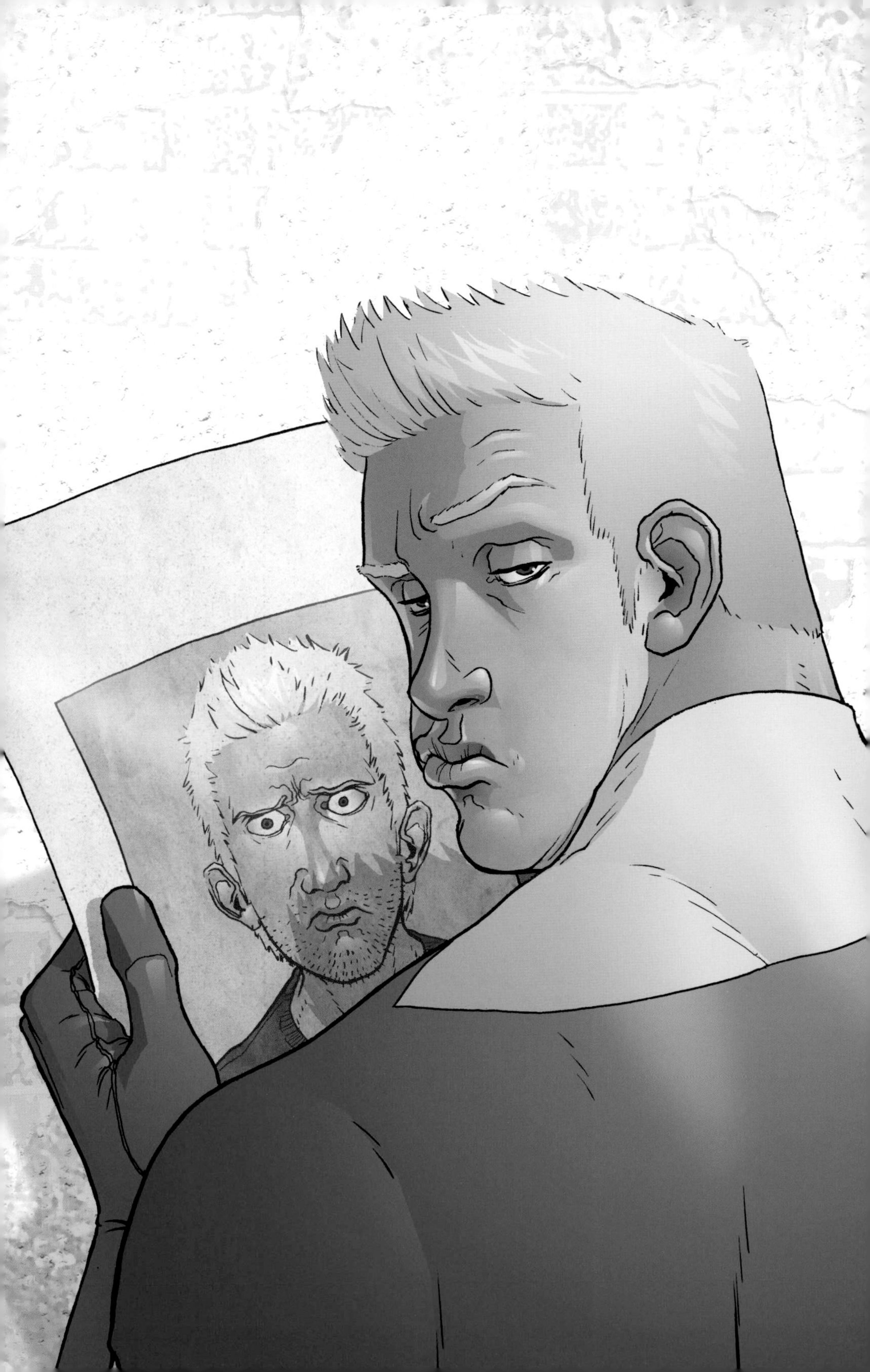

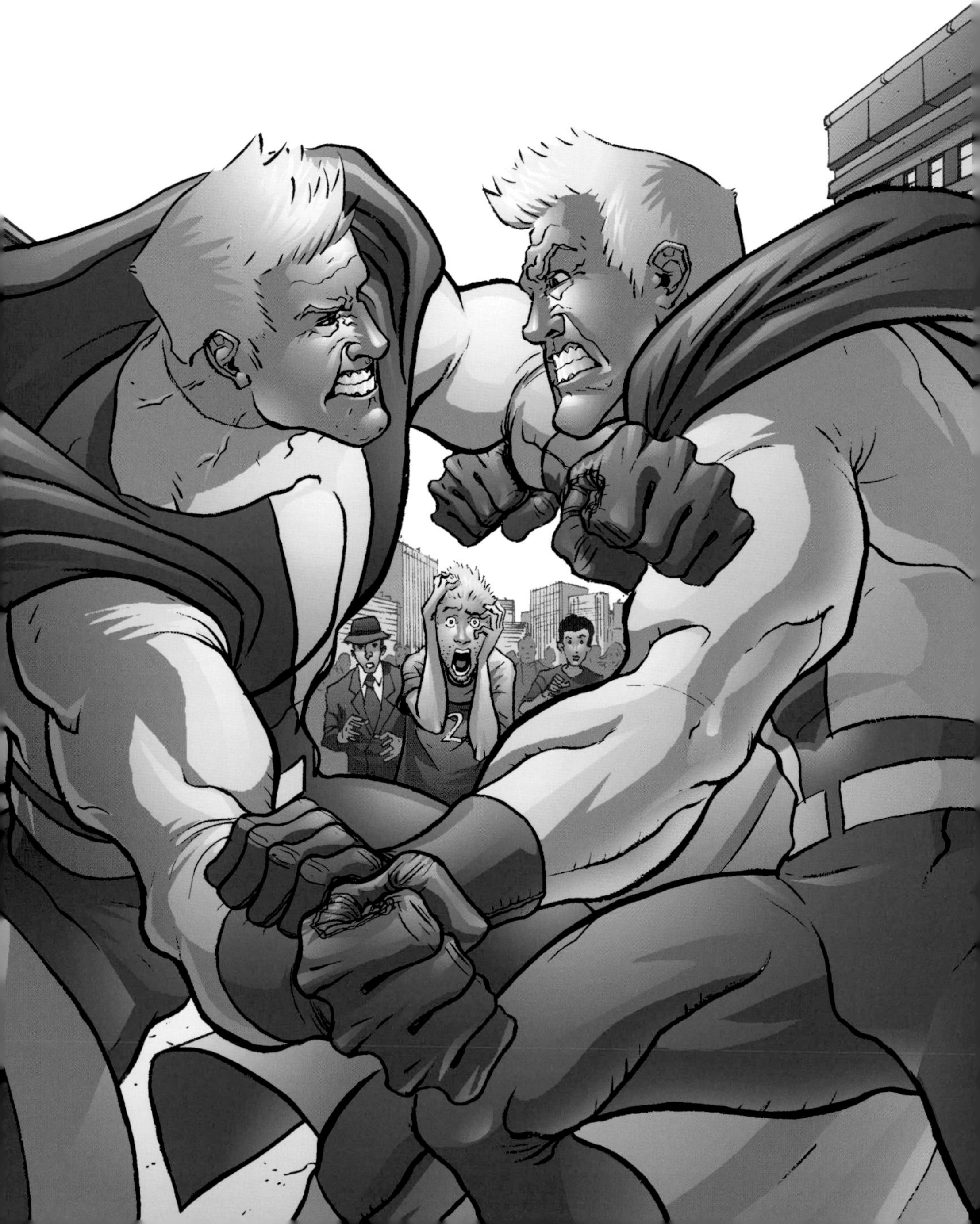

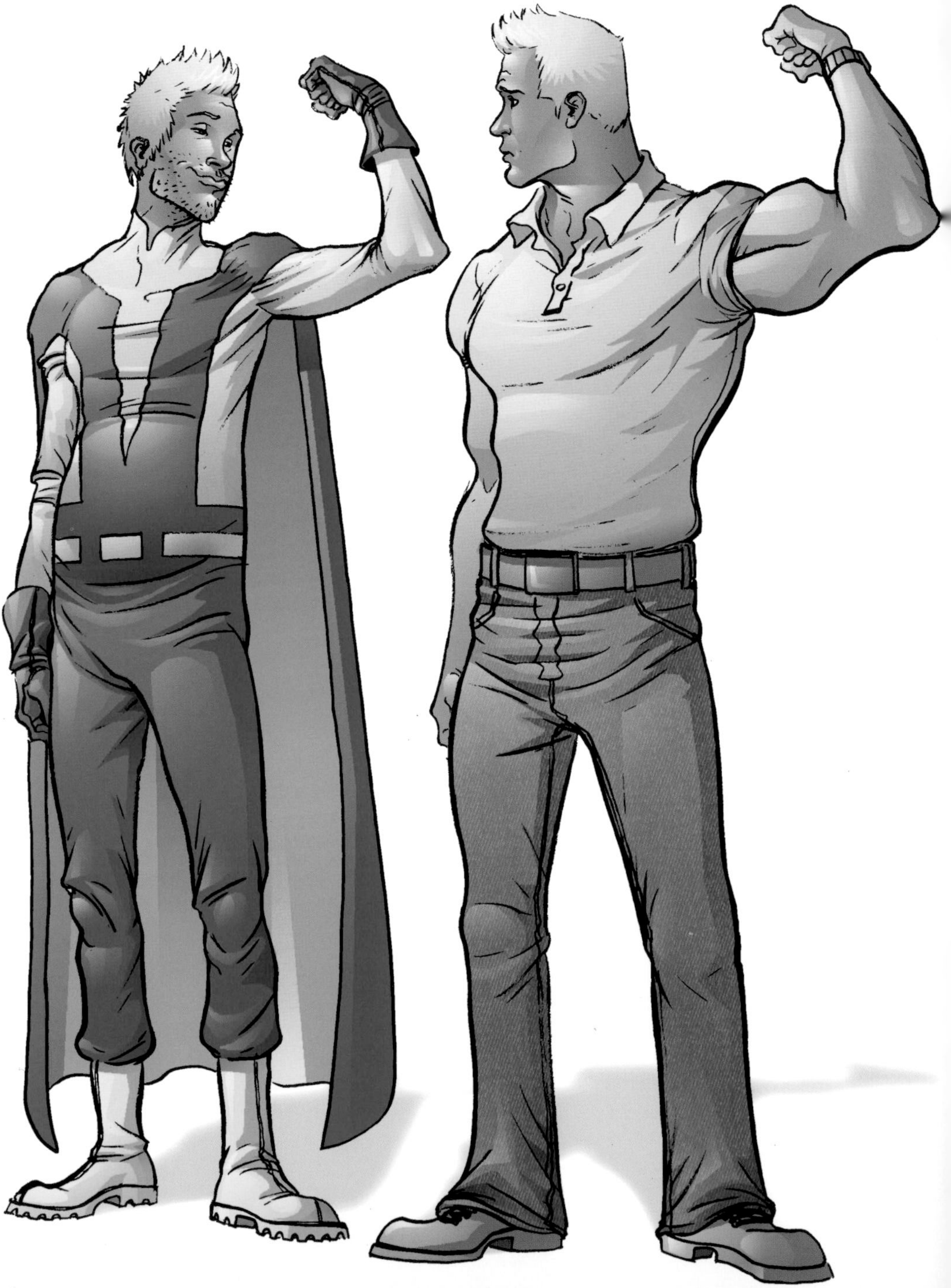

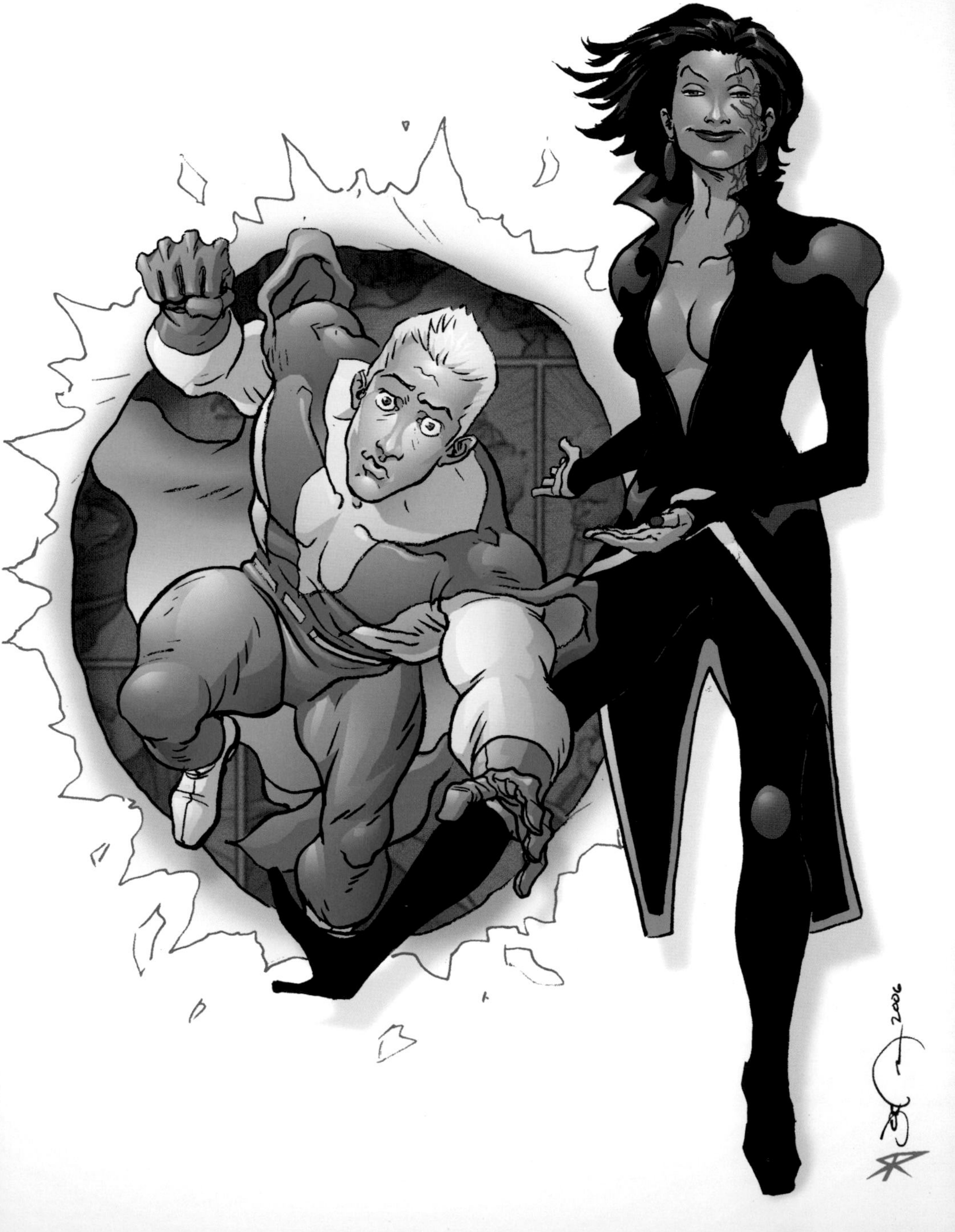
2006